ALEXIS SOYER
COOK EXTRAORDINARY

Soyer as the cook 'Mirobolant', caricature by W. M. Thackeray in Pendennis, *1850*

ALEXIS SOYER

COOK

EXTRAORDINARY

by
ELIZABETH RAY

with a foreword by Prue Leith

SOUTHOVER PRESS
1991

First published 1991 by
SOUTHOVER PRESS
2, Cockshut Road, Lewes, East Sussex BN7 1JH
Copyright © Text Elizabeth Ray
© Foreword Prue Leith
A catalogue record for this book is available
from the British Library
ISBN 1-870962-05-2
Phototypeset in Palatino 11/13 by City Marketing, Chichester
Printed in England on wood-free paper by
Villiers Publications Ltd, 26A Shepherds Hill, London N6 5AH
for Southover Press

All rights reserved. No part of this publication may be reproduced, stored in a retrieval system, or transmitted, in any form, or by any means, electronic, mechanical, photocopying, recording or otherwise, without the prior permission of the publishers.

Contents

Sources of Illustrations — vi
Author's Note — viii
Acknowledgements — viii
Foreword — ix
1. SETTING THE SCENE — 1
2. THE REFORMING CHEF — 21
3. A BROTH OF A BOY — 43
4. SOYER AT LARGE — 59
5. COOKS AND BOOKS — 69
6. STOVES AND SAUCES — 97
7. THE EXHIBITIONIST — 109
8. CULINARY CAMPAIGN — 125
9. FAREWELL, SOYER — 155
10. RECIPES — 159
Select Bibliography — 176
Index — 177

Sources of Illustrations

From the Mary Evans Picture Library, illustrations on pages 1, 23, 26, 27, 34, 45, 48, 52, 57, 102, 103, 114, 136, 149.

From Dick Doyles Diary, illustrations on pages 4, 60, 69.

From *Punch*, p. 42.

From *The Modern Housewife*, illustrations on pages ii, 58, 79, 96, 103, 124, 158, 179.

From the Witt Library, Courtauld Institute, page 20.

From The Mansell Collection, pages 13, 117.

From *Pendennis*, W.M. Thackeray, drawing by W.M. Thackeray, frontispiece.

From *The Gastronomic Regenerator*, illustrations on pages 16, 17, 26, 27, 38, 39, 63, 70, 88, 99, 159.

From *Shilling Cookery for the People*, illustrations on pages 49, 108, 167, 181.

From *The Culinary Campaign*, illustrations on pages 91, 130, 133, 145.

*This is for Joan Bailey,
one-time colleague, life-time friend,
who helped so much with the research*

Acknowledgements

I have received information and help from many sources, particularly from the Reform Club; the Florence Nightingale Museum; the Army Catering Corps; the Public Record Office; the National Voluntary Civil Aid Services, and the invaluable London Library.

I am especially grateful to Michael McKirdy, of Cooks' Books, Rottingdean; to Amanda-Jane Doran, of the *Punch* Library, and to Linda Doyle for her efficient typing.

Author's Note

This is not an in-depth biography. It is an account of the work of a man who has long interested me, and I hope will interest others as well.

I have tried to set him against the contemporary background and have quoted extensively from newspapers and journals of the time. Other quotations, unless indicated differently, come from Soyer's own works, or the *Memoirs of Soyer* written by his secretaries, Messrs Volant and Warren. Although Soyer uses the word receipt in describing his menus, I have used the more familiar word recipe in the text.

Foreword

It is surprising how few books have been written about Alexis Soyer. With his energy, eccentricity and vanity, and his truly extraordinary life, he would seem the answer to a biographer's prayer. But what there has been up to now is poor stuff—a near contemporary memoir by his two secretaries which is almost unreadable in its sycophancy and pomposity, and a rather pedestrian *Portrait of a Chef* by Helen Morris published in 1938.

But at last we have a writer fit for the task and prepared to devote her talents to "a mere cook". Elizabeth Ray is exactly that writer. She has a lightness of style which makes reading about Victorian life as easy as reading a gossip column and it is happily combined with a scholarly dedication to fact and an affectionate enthusiasm for her subject.

And what a subject! *The Globe* of 1841 wrote "The impression grows on us that the man of his age is neither Sir Robert Peel, nor Lord John Russell, or even Ibrahim Pasha, but Alexis Soyer." Even by Victorian standards, when hyperbole and exaggeration were common currency, the statement is justified. Soyer's fame was not occasioned only by his illustrious dinners for the fashionable at the Reform Club and elsewhere, though there were plenty of these. He gave, unpaid, two years of his life to revolutionising the Scutari hospital kitchens in the Crimea, doing for nutrition what Florence Nightingale was doing for nursing. He raised the money for and personally organised soup kitchens during the Irish famine and for the destitute silk workers in Spitalfields. His determination to make the rich notice the poor, and provide for them, made him the Bob Geldof of his day, albeit better dressed.

FOREWORD

A bold entrepreneur and consummate salesman, he set up, in 1851, a rival attraction to the Great Exhibition. This was a multi-restaurant 'theme-park'—a precursor of Disneyworld for rich gourmet and modest worker. It consisted of Chinese Gardens, tropical palms, the world's architectural wonders (leaning tower of Pisa, Eddystone Lighthouse, etc.), picture galleries, ice caverns complete with double-glass windows with swimming fish between the panes, entertainments from ballooning to African dancing, and food to satisfy every nation "civilised or uncivilised" on earth, drawing the line only at feeding "ebony-skinned and boomeranged chieftains" with "baked young woman for two, with a cold boiled missionary to follow". The combination of exuberance, vulgarity and good food attracted people by the thousand.

A man of extraordinary practical talents, absolutely nothing daunted Soyer. He designed one of the first gas kitchens, portable stoves for the military, ships' galleys, the waiter's flame lamp, coffee pots, tea-urns and much more.

Mrs Ray reveals a side to Soyer that I've always suspected but never had confirmed. Like many a cook of his day—and indeed today—honesty was a moveable feast. He was frequently in trouble with the Reform Club committees about butchers' bills and kitchen expenses. Mrs Ray's researches have revealed a bit of serious dishonesty that I can't help finding eminently satisfactory. *The Pantropheon, or a history of food and its preparation in ancient times* is an enormous book covering the farming, manufacture, ingredients, and cuisines of antiquity. It is obviously the result of years', if not a lifetime's, work. To me at least, it is almost unreadable, and I am relieved and delighted to learn from Mrs Ray that Soyer never wrote it. He was paid by its French author, a monsieur Duhart-Fauvet, to translate it, but passed it off as his own. Disgraceful I agree. But it does explain the unSoyer-like pedantry of the work, quite unlike his other books.

Soyer was a relentless practical joker and bonviveur. He invented a morning suit that, at the pull of a string, was transformed into evening wear so that he could embarrass his hostess by turning up ill-suited, then put the matter right, to hoots of admiring laughter. His usual dress was anyway eccentric, flamboyant, and sometimes wildly over the top. He had once contemplated a singing career—he had a find voice. And his love of the theatre had him designing pantomime transformation scenes and writing a ballet—sadly undanceable.

Elizabeth Ray manages to build a picture of Soyer that acknowledges him to be insufferably vain and publicity-seeking, but reveals also the devoted husband, the dedicated chef—to be found at Hungerford market choosing lobsters, or orchestrating an open-air ox-roast in Exeter castle yard —and the campaigning author writing best-selling cookery books for the poor, and drumming up money to feed them.

Soyer's is a fascinating character, and he lived at a time absolutely suited to him. The Victorians appreciated and lionised larger-than-life characters, and Soyer was up there in the Pantheon with Dickens, Isambard Brunel and Disraeli. That his name has, unlike theirs, ceased to be widely known, is not because he does not deserve a place in history. He does, though perhaps not quite such a large or limelit place as he would like, but a niche at least. And with any luck this most readable and excellent book will ensure him that.

PRUE LEITH

God save our jolly chef,
Long live our noble chef
    God save Soyer!
Crimea victorious,
Always victorious
To join in our choreus,
    God save Soyer!

Oh, Ude, Vatel, arise,
Try Soyer's pigeon pies,
    And fricandeaux!
Confound their mayonnaise,
On him we throw our praise,
And worship his entremets,
    God save Soyer!

His choicest wine in store
On us he's pleased to pour,
    Long will we drink!
May he into our paws
Hand crab and lobster claws,
Gaining our whole applause,
    God save Soyer!

Sung at a dinner given to Soyer after his return from the Crimea, and reproduced in the *Memoirs of Soyer* by Volant and Warren.

Meaux-en-Brie, early nineteenth century

Setting the Scene

In 1831 an obscure young French cook left Paris to work in England. This was to be his home for the rest of his life, and he was to become a national figure.

Alexis Benoist Soyer was born in 1809, in the small town of Meaux-en-Brie, not far from Paris, famous for its cheese. His family were shopkeepers, and they wanted Alexis, the youngest of their three sons, to go into the Church. He was sent as a chorister to the local cathedral school, where his uncle, the Grand Vicar, accepted him as a pupil with the intention that eventually he would be admitted as a priest.

But Alexis, although he had a good voice and enjoyed the singing, could not accept the strict regime and spent too much of his time playing practical jokes. His series of pranks ended after he, and some friends, rang the church bells late one night; as these also served as a fire alarm for the town and a signal for the town garrison to muster, much confusion followed, with the result that young Alexis was expelled from the seminary.

He had no strong idea as to where his future lay, and in the end accepted the suggestion of his elder brother Phillipe, established as a chef in Paris, that he should follow the same profession, and he was apprenticed to various well-known restaurants in Paris. He did very well, and by the time he was seventeen had been appointed head of the kitchen at the restaurant Douix, in the Boulevard des Italiens, where he had a dozen cooks under him; a big responsibility for such a young man.

He must have been a bit of a handful for his elder brother to cope with, as he was as much interested in the stage and in singing as in his cooking. However he continued to improve his skills with such good effect that at the age of twenty he was appointed second cook to the French Foreign Office, for which he had to prepare many formal banquets.

This was when France was in another revolutionary period, that which saw the end of the Bourbon regime and introduced the house of Orleans, when Louis Philippe was made king.

It was during this time, when Alexis Soyer was busy preparing a special banquet for the then Foreign Minister, the Prince Polignac, that some revolutionaries broke into the Foreign Office through the kitchen, shooting as they did so and, among others, killing two of the cooks. Soyer claimed afterwards that he was only saved by his presence of mind and his good voice, as he jumped on to a table and began to sing La Marseillaise very loudly, and amid the cheers this brought forth was able to get away.

By that time Philippe Soyer had come to England to work as chef to the Duke of Cambridge, and after the episode with the revolutionaries he persuaded Alexis to join him, which was how he came to this country, which he then adopted as his own.

SETTING THE SCENE

Alexis Soyer was very much a man of his time – flamboyant, inventive, revolutionary in some things, conventional in others, he enjoyed the good life, yet was concerned about others less fortunate – he fitted in easily to the England which was "characterised by such constant and rapid changes in economic circumstances, social custom and intellectual atmosphere", for this was the era of the Industrial Revolution, with its inventions, reforms and new wealth making the country change from the extravagances of the Regency time to the more sedate virtues of the Victorian age. It was an age that is much more familiar to us today, with modern inventions and appliances such as the railway system, gas for lighting and cooking, electricity, photography and the telegraph system all having their beginnings at this time. It was an age of great expansion, culminating in the Great Exhibition of 1851, where all these new technical advances were shown proudly to the world.

The wars with Napoleon were over, and no others threatened, so it was a time when Britain could concentrate on changes within herself, not least of which was the rise of the middle classes and the consequent reorganisation of the whole British social scene.

This was the time of growth of the Trade Unions, factory reforms, better education, including education for adults, and friendly benefit societies. It was also the time for agricultural riots, machine-breaking, anti-Poor-Law, anti-Corn-Law activities, and Chartism, with its ideas of self-help and independence. All indicative of the wish of the people to change their lot, and the lot of others less well placed, and to take advantage of the new opportunities offered. The first Reform Bill which came in 1832, did not have great immediate effect, but showed that the idea of reform was accepted and changes desirable.

The invention that probably had more impact than any other single factor on the changes taking place, was the growth of the railway system. Railways had started experimentally as a way of moving coal from the pits to the factories, but gradually became essential for carrying other goods, and were only later used for passengers. The speed with which a journey could be completed, compared to the old horse-drawn coaches, opened up the countryside to an exciting degree, and by the 1840s there was a national railway network which, along with the development of the Electric Telegraph Company and the Penny Post, revolutionised the whole communication system of the country.

Surtees, in his way as vivid a chronicler of the times as Dickens was, wrote of these changes, "In truth, the country gentlemen were a land-locked, leg-tied tribe before the introduction of the railways – coaching was uncomfortable, andposting expensive, beside which a journey took such a time. There was no running up to town for a week in those days. It took the best part of a week coming from remote country to make the journey and recover from the effects of it. No wonder the gentry did not make them very often, and contented themselves with their country towns instead of the capital. They were somebody in them, but nobody when they got to London." And he goes on to describe another of the innovations of the time: "the establishment of the Penny Post,

and liberal scattering of Post-Offices too, had been a wonderful boon to country gentlemen, indeed to all sorts and condition of people; but the old squires being about the only people in the country who received letters, or who, perhaps could read them when got, were often sadly put to in the sending long distances for them. The grand, the crowning benefit of all, however, were railways. Without them cheap postage, cheap papers, cheap literature, extended post-offices, would have been inefficient, for the old coaches would never have carried the quantity of matter modern times have evoked." (*Plain or Ringlets*.)

Of course not everyone welcomed the railways. The coachmen resented this new-fangled method of travel – even if their passengers would have preferred it. Soyer himself gives an account, in the *Culinary Campaign*, of a journey from Windsor to Virginia Water, which went well as far as Staines, as he went by special train, the journey taking twenty-five minutes. Then he had to board the coach: "We were now at full trot, the north wind in our faces, and a kind of heavy sleet, which in a few minutes changed the colour of our noses to a deep crimson, very much like the unfashionable colour of beetroot, freezing our whiskers and moustaches like sugar-candy, but by no means quite so sweet-tasted. By way of a joke, I said to the coachman, 'This is the good old English way of travelling, is it not?' 'That it is, sir; and I'm very glad to see you know how to appreciate it. Talk about your railways, it's perfect nonsense compared with a good four-in-hand coach sir . . . I recollect the good old time when we took from fourteen to fifteen hours from London to Dover, changing horses and drinking your glass of grog at almost every inn on the road . . . then you really knew if you were travelling or stopping at home; while now they pack you up under lock and key, in strong wooden boxes, such as we keep our horses in at the stable; and at the head of them they have a kind of long iron saveloy, full of nothing, which runs away with the lot like mad, belching and swearing all the way, taking sights at us poor coachmen just so,' putting his hand to his nose, 'when we go by, as though we were a set of ragamuffins. Call that a gentlemanly way of travelling, sir!'"

The new developments, particularly the greater mobility that the railways gave, and the prosperity of the factories and mills contributed to the rise of the new middle classes. They were to a great extent city people, who got their greater social standing from their interests in manufacturing, mining and ship building, with the increased wealth these produced. The new class grew from the inventions and commerce of the nineteenth century, and there was another new breed, too, of factory workers, often labourers who moved from the country to the towns wherever work was offered, as did the 'Navvies' – navigators who worked on the canals, but now moved to the railway.

Until this time it had been fairly well defined in the British social system who was a 'Gentleman' and who was not. The new affluence of the factory and mill owner meant that there was a blurring of some of these distinctions. The land owning class remained the gentry, but as more and more people acquired money and a steadily increasing income, they were able to buy land and assume some of the manners and customs of the higher class. To become acceptable "an income above a certain minimum was the first requisite. A particular occupation or calling was also useful in identifying a person as middle class. Education, religious affiliation and style of home provided further distinguishing characteristics. Even so, within these limits wide differences in wealth and status were possible, and it is therefore convenient to distinguish between the *haute bourgeoisie* and the lower middle class. The very top level of the middle classes lived on terms of familiarity with the aristocracy, and, as we have seen, inter-married with them. London bankers and City merchants were some of the wealthiest people in the country, and together with their provincial counterparts form a small financial oligarchy. The industrial magnates dominated the regional scene: coal and iron masters in South Wales, mill owners in Yorkshire and Lancashire, engineers and ship builders in Liverpool and Scotland. By the early Victorian period these men of business and industry had founded dynasties." (Harrison: *The Early Victorians 1832–1851.*)

Property of some kind was essential for the new middle classes, building societies helped to finance home ownership, and this became a social step upwards. If it was not possible to have a home of one's own, material goods such as solid mahogany furniture, silver, a piano, and at least one domestic servant, were all on show to emphasise the rise in status, and there was a gradual change from chapel to church worship. Further down the social scale the increase in cultural habits and ideas meant that the artisans gradually became clerks and shopkeepers, and the idea of a labouring poor gave way to that of a working class, and so everyone took a step upwards.

There was also of course the dark side to all this prosperity. It was at this time that Disraeli, in his novel *Sybil* identified "the Two Nations" – a phrase that we hear often again nowadays, – and other novelists, Dickens, of course, and Mrs Gaskell, particularly in her *Mary Barton* and *North and South*, gave a vivid picture of the good and the bad in this age of industrial revolution, and Mrs Oliphant showed the snobbery and great divide between the church goers and chapel people.

All this movement of labour produced problems in the way of poor housing, slums, changes in traditional ways of living, and, of major importance, something from which this country has never really recovered; changes in the diet. In her book *Food in England*, Dorothy Hartley describes some of these consequences: "With the Industrial Revolution the people were driven off the land; they are cut off from their natural food supply, and are compelled for the first time to buy food. The cruelty of the Industrial Revolution was that it made money a necessity of *life*; it is not the crowding into towns, to work in the factories, not the land, neglected, ceasing to provide food, *it is a dislocation of the food supply*.

"Townspeople today rarely realise the necessary continuity of country work. On the land one must wait three years before it is possible to live; it is corn bought two years previously that is today's bread, beef is two years, or more, agrowing, one ewe, even if she has twin lambs, must suckle and graze them into the second year before mutton is available; even the cheaply bought runkling pig must be well fed for months before it is slaughtered, and without the year's work and growth in the field, there is nothing to feed the pig! This is elementary, yet so many people say unthinkingly, "Why did they not return to the country?" The 'country' is like a door that slams shut!

"Only country people realise the impossibility of leaving the land, for even a few months, without losing all livelihood from it for at least a year. For the unfortunate victims of the industrial townships, there was no 'return home'. Once away from their basic proportion of arable land, they were dependent, for the first time in history."

The British Isles do not differ so greatly in climate from the far North to the South, so that, in general, the same kind of foodstuff can be grown and eaten, unlike France, for example, with such a great difference in style and climate between the Channel and the Mediterranean. It seems that here the differences are still more between the town and country, and with the drift to the towns in the early nineteenth century this became more noticeable, and both urban and rural life suffered. The national diet changed and has never gone back to the previous pattern. As Dorothy Hartley also wrote: "It is difficult for the historian housekeeper to explain the divide between poverty and wealth, and good food and poor food; they are not the same division. In early English history the division between the enormously wealthy and powerful, and completely penniless multitude, is not a division of food. The over lord might feast, and the hireling fast, but both could do it on the same basic English materials... A countryman's family, even under the most slavish conditions, often had as good food as their own industry could provide *for themselves*. The wool on his back, the leather shoes on his feet, the pork in his larder, and corn in his bin, were a man's own growing, . ."

What happened at this time of the growth of factories, mills, ship-yards and so on, was that the town diets were inadequate and boring, consisting mainly of bread, potatoes and tea. More and more women went out to work in the factories so that food had to be prepared as and when they were at home and a fire was available, or taken to the nearest baker, who would cook it, for a charge, in his cooling oven after the bread was made. (There were many abuses of this system, not least a baker 'losing' a dish that had been brought in, and Punch defined an honest baker as one who buys his own Sunday dinner.) Street vendors were busy at this time selling prepared simple food – the take-away is nothing new – and in London especially, cold fried flounder was a popular delicacy. So were hot baked potatoes, and it wasn't long before someone had the idea of putting these two commodities together, and there came the ever popular fish-and-chip shops.

Staple foods changed quite radically over the years, and many traditions were lost. Because milk was sent to the towns the country people were unable to get as much as they were used to. In the North, for example, where dishes based on oatmeal were common, if there was no milk the oatmeal was too unappetising to eat, and except for Scotland where the population was sparse, its use greatly diminished.

The other side of this change in diet was that the better-off had a much wider range of fruit, spices, country produce such as butter and eggs, and, owing to the speed with which the railways could deliver fresh food, inland areas were now assured of a good supply of fish, which they had never had before. By 1848 seventy tons of fish were sent every week from East Anglian ports to London to make a new trade and a new diet for many people. The pattern of sending fish to London from these ports and then on to the provinces is still in operation, and even if one lives near the coast it is sometimes difficult to get fish that hasn't come by way of the London markets. The best haddock landed at Grimsby and smoked there used to be, and perhaps still is, called London haddock, as being destined for Billingsgate.

Until the railways altered the face, and the diet, of the country, most food would have been locally grown and sold in the local market town. But there was also an expansion of shops in the country as well as the bigger towns, and although regional differences remained to some extent, there was a wider range of foods available nationally.

Another very significant change in the social scene, and not possible before the advent of the railways, was the emergence of the London Club, and this had a great significance for Alexis Soyer who became the first chef to the Reform Club, created in 1837. Surtees, in his *Plain or Ringlets*, explains why they were so important: "The next greatest boon to railways that modern squires have to be thankful for, is the great multiplication of London Clubs. Without Clubs, the railway system would have been incomplete. After such luxurious travelling a man requires something better than the old coaching houses – the Bull-and-Mouth, the Golden Cross, or even the once-prized Piazza, with its large cabbage-smelling coffee-rooms . . . the railway companies, to be sure, anticipated the want, and built spacious hotels at their respective termini, the Piazza became a Crystal Palace, and the Bull-and-Mouth changed its ugly name! But disguise it as you will, an hotel is an hotel, and an Englishman cannot make himself believe it is his home.

"Then these railway houses are all out of the way of where pleasure-seeking people want to be and though a party's requirements are fairly supplied, yet these hotels hold out no inducement for a run up to town for the mere pleasure of the thing. This is what Clubs do. They invite visits. A man feels that he has a real substantial home – a home containing every imaginable luxury, without the trouble of management or forethought – a home that goes on as steadily in his absence as during his presence, to which he has not even the trouble of writing a note to say he is coming, to find everything as comfortable as he left it . . . Although the country gentlemen have become a very different race to what they were. They are more men of the world . . . Whether this change is attributable to the emancipation of railways, or to the shock their system sustained by the ruthless repeal of the Corn-laws, or a combination of both, is immaterial to inquire."

* * * * *

SETTING THE SCENE

This, then, was the sort of England that the young Frenchman came to live in during the first part of the nineteenth century. A country of new ideas, new inventions, new class structures, extremes of riches and poverty and a changing countryside. And where he was to make his mark in many different ways.

When Alexis Soyer first came to England he joined his brother in the household of the Duke of Cambridge, but soon went off on his own and worked in other grand houses. One of the places where he was very happy working was at Aston Hall, a fine house just outside Oswestry, belonging to a Mr William Lloyd. He stayed there for several years and became not only famous for his cooking, but also became something of a local character, and according to the *Memoirs of Soyer* (written by his secretaries, and recently republished by Cook's Books) "many of the leading aristocracy when giving entertainments eagerly sought his assistance. Among the many epicures of those days, Myddleton Biddulph, esq., lord of Chirk Castle, did not disdain to partake of the fruits of our hero's culinary lore ... during his hours of leisure he was always the life and soul of every convivial party to which he was invited, and at many of the dinners at which he has been present as a welcome guest, he has been merely partaking of his own productions."

The railways must have played a major part in the lives of such landowners and epicures. Not only were they able to attract and keep such staff as Soyer, but because of the greater ease of communication between town and country it meant that not only could important guests be brought to the house to stay, but, as important from the chef's point of view, good raw materials were available for the kitchen. The increase in the variety and quality of food that could be obtained in such places must have been astonishing to those who, up to that time, had had to rely on whatever could be produced and bought locally.

After he left Mr Lloyd's service he went for a time to the Marquis of Ailsa as chef, and presumably he met many influential people there, so it is not surprising that he was appointed chef to the newly formed Reform Club, and it was here, where he worked for twelve years, that he made his reputation, both as chef to the rich and cook to the poor. It is clear that he quickly made a reputation as a good companion, and he was witty, kind-hearted, hard-working, and really quite vain. He also was an incurable joker, which must have tried his friends a good deal. He dressed in an extravagant manner, full of his own quirky mannerisms, and as the *Memoirs* put it, he was "Generous in the extreme, and not altogether free from ostentation."

He wore gold-braided waistcoats, diamond rings, a hat that was made so that it would not sit straight on his head, but was always worn *à la zoug-zoug*, and later on in his life he adopted this zigzag cut in other clothes as well – he once had a suit made so that although it looked like a morning suit at first, by one flick of the wrist it converted to evening dress; he sometimes kept money in specially built heels to his dress boots, and had visiting cards made diamond-shaped instead of the conventional rectangle, and his writing sloped forwards, except for his signature which sloped the other way.

Thackeray, who later became a good friend and admirer of Soyer, caricatured him in his novel *Pendennis* by describing the cook he called Mirabolant: "He walked . . . in his usual favourite costume, namely, his light green frock or paletot, his crimson velvet waistcoat with blue glass buttons, his pantalo Ecossais of a very large and decided check pattern, his orange satin neckcloth, and his jean-boots, with tips of shiny leather, – these, with a gold-embroidered cap, and a richly-gilt cane, or other varieties of ornament of a similar tendency, formed his usual holiday costume, in which he flattered himself there was nothing remarkable (unless, indeed, the beauty of his person should attract observation), and in which he considered that he exhibited the appearance of a gentleman of good parisian ton."

Although he went out of his way to appear unconventional and ostentatious, nevertheless he was extremely serious about his profession. George Augustus Sala, a journalist, artist and gourmet, who helped Soyer design his Grand Symposium at the time of the Great Exhibition in 1851, recalled how he first came across Soyer in Hungerford Market: " 'Who can that extraordinary individual be?' I asked my brother. The stranger was a stoutish, tallish gentleman, a little past middle age, with closely cropped grey hair and a stubby grey moustache; and, but for his more than peculiar costume, he might have been mistaken for the riding-master of a foreign circus, who had originally been in the army. He wore a kind of paletot of light camlet cloth, with voluminous lapels and deep cuffs of lavender watered silk; very baggy trousers, with a lavender stripe down the seams; very shiny boots, and quite as glossy a hat; his attire being completed by tightly-fitting gloves, of the hue known in Paris as *buerre frais* – that is to say, light yellow. All this you may think was odd enough; but an extraordinary oddity was added to his appearance by the circumstances that

George Augustus Sala

was cut on what the dressmakers call a 'bias', or as he himself, when I came to know him well, used to designate as *à la zoug-zoug*. He must have been the terror of his tailor, his hatter, and his maker of cravats and underlinen; since he had, to all appearances an unconquerable aversion from any garment which, when displayed on the human figure, exhibited either horizontal or perpendicular lines. His very visiting-cards, his cigar-case, and the handle of his cane took slightly oblique inclinations.

"He evidently knew all about shell-fish; for he took the lobsters up one by one, critically scanned them, poised them in one hand after the other to ascertain their weight, examined their claws, rapped them on their back, poked their sides, and offered terms for them in a mildly authoritative tone; terms whi ch were at length, and not very ruefully, accepted by the fishmonger, who was possibly desirous of keeping on the best terms with the foreign gentleman whose hat, coat, cravat, and pantaloons were all so studiously awry. 'Who is that?' said my brother, repeating my question. 'Why, of all people on earth, who could that be but Soyer?"

This meeting took place, of course, when he was well established, but although he appeared past middle age and with grey hair, he cannot yet have been forty.

Soyer had to be in the limelight, it is true, but he worked tirelessly, and not always for money. He understood the importance of a good diet, and although he made his living by cooking for the rich, a good deal of time was spent in seeing that the less well-off were adequately fed as well. This was the era of Victorian benevolence and charity to the poor, but whereas many benefactors contented themselves with just providing money and "improving" the poor with religious tracts, Soyer turned his practical mind to the best way of feeding them, and he wrote books, not only for his aristocratic patrons, but also for the middle and working classes. His mind was always working to think up some new dish, joke, invention, excuse for fun – but let the *Memoirs* sum him up: ". . . how he revelled in luxurious mental images, and made

SETTING THE SCENE

human nature's mouth water! As fast as one invention grew stale, out came another; magic kitchens, gas cooking apparatuses, cottagers' stoves, aerial stoves, magic coffee-pot, egg-cooking machines, ballet, and various books on cookery; relishes and sauces of all kinds, celebrated nectar, mustard of delectable flavour; his pineapple punch and punch *à la Marmora*, all of which will be entered into. One could write upon them for a week; but let us not anticipate."

* * * * *

By the time he was twenty-six, Soyer had become established in England and was highly regarded in his profession, and he considered it was about time he got married. He had an old love in Paris – as we shall learn later on – and he thought it would be a good idea to send her a portrait of himself, to find presumably, whether she would still consider him or not.

He made enquiries about a suitable painter for this portrait and was recommended to a Monsieur Simonau, Flemish by birth, but who lived and worked in London. He went to visit M. Simonau and was then introduced to one of his pupils, Emma Jones, aged twenty-two, who was making quite a name for herself as a portraitist.

Emma's father had died when she was only a few years old, and her mother devoted herself to bringing up the child as best she could, which included seeing that she had lessons in both painting and music. Originally her mother wanted her to concentrate on the music, but after she had sent the girl as a pupil to M. Simonau, who thought highly of her talents, she agreed to let her concentrate on the painting. Perhaps the fact that in 1820, when Emma was seven, Mrs Jones married M. Simonau had a lot to do with the decision. Anyway, whatever the reason, she became quite well established as a painter, particularly of portraits, and had successful exhibitions in several galleries.

Alexis Soyer, by his wife

She agreed to paint Soyer's portrait, during which time they fell in love, and eventually, in spite of some opposition from her step-father, who although he liked Soyer, disapproved of Emma marrying *a cook*, they were married at St George's, Hanover Square, in April 1837. One of the witnesses at the ceremony was Louis Eustache Ude, one of the most celebrated chefs at the time, and one who was a firm friend and mentor of the young Alexis.

Emma must have been a charming and lively person, – there is a self-portrait of her in Soyer's book *The Gastronomic Regenerator*, – and well able to keep up with Soyer's endless jokes and witticisms. There is a pleasing story of how, during

Emma Soyer, by herself

the courtship, Soyer sent her a bunch of flowers, only to find that he got a parcel back, with a very formal note from Emma, saying that if he insisted in sending her such things he would only find them returned to him. Alexis was very disconsolate at what he thought must be a rebuff, but when he opened the parcel he found not the flowers he had sent, but a charming painting of them. She also wrote the "Fashionable Precept for the Ladies"; which included the following advice:

> "To speak naturally, to act naturally, are vulgar and commonplace in the extreme.
> To move and think as you feel inclined are offences that

no polite person can ever in honour or delicacy forgive.

In walking keep your feet extended out nearly to a right angle with your body, and seldom let more than the points of your toes touch the ground.

Keep your shoulders at the same time well extended back; and, in a word, during the whole of your gait, suppose yourself to be anything but what you are.

Take your meals invariably later than your vulgar neighbours.

Go to bed at two in the morning, and rise at twelve the next day. You will then become a fashionable lady, and, in the midst of congratulation, you will entirely forget the sacrifice of truth and nature by which you have acquired this enviable distinction."

And a lot more in the same vein. I don't know if these words were ever published, or if so where. They would have hardly made her popular with her own sex, but I doubt if she would have minded that.

On one occasion, when Soyer was working at the Reform Club, Emma called to see him for some reason, but he was very busy at the time, and after waiting for over an hour, she called one of the Club servants and said that she had waited long enough, but had left her card. What she had done was to sketch a self-portrait on the wall, which so pleased Soyer when he eventually came out to find her, that he had a frame and glass put over it, and the drawing was preserved for years. Alas, it is no longer there.

She was a prolific painter and left enough pictures behind her after her early death, for Soyer to mount an exhibition of them to raise money for the poor silk weavers of Spitalfields, who were among the poorest of the skilled workers, and for whom Soyer established one of his soup kitchens. She was sometimes described as the "English Murillo", and specialised in paintings of children in natural settings, not so much the studio portrait. Some of her best known works were "The Young Israelites", "The English Ceres", and "Alpine Wanderers", a picture of two boys, one playing with a hurdy-gurdy, and the other with some white mice. This particular picture was sold for 100 guineas, which in those days was a considerable sum. She painted a charming portrait of Alexis, showing him wearing his cap, *à la zoug-zoug*, and smiling as he starts to eat a chicken leg. In this picture he looks far more natural and at ease than in any of the other portraits of him.

Her work was well received by the critics, several of whom decided that she was painting under a pseudonym, and following an exhibition at the Louvre where she had several pictures on show, one critic wrote "what we consider most singular is, that no woman ever painted with so much vigour and ease. Madame Soyer (supposing always that Madame Soyer is a woman) is to the other painters what George Sand is to literary men." Over-praise perhaps, but she was obviously taken seriously.

She was very keen to exhibit at the Royal Academy, and applied to the President to be allowed to do so, obviously not realising that this was not the correct approach, and when she received a formal refusal from the authorities there she was deeply distressed and humiliated. However the British Institution, a gallery founded at the beginning of the century to exhibit British artists, was happy to show many of her paintings. This Institution lasted for about sixty years, until the lease on the house in Pall Mall, almost opposite the Reform Club where Alexis worked, ran out.   In 1842, Alexis was invited to go to Belgium to visit the Duke of Saxe-Coburg, brother of the King of the Belgians who was a great admirer both of Soyer as a chef, and Emma as a painter. Emma was heavily pregnant at the time so was not able to go with Alexis, so he took a couple of her paintings with him to show his host, and left Emma to finish the portrait she was working on, and expected to be back in plenty of time before the baby arrived.

Unfortunately while he was away there was a terrific thunder-storm in London, and poor Emma, left alone in the house in her very pregnant condition, was so terrified that she miscarried, and died the next day. She was only 29.

Alexis had the news broken to him by his secretary who went immediately to Brussels to see him, and bring him home.

He was deeply upset, the more so as he felt that if he had not gone away she would have been all right, and he felt not only grief but guilt – feelings that never really left him. One of his old employers, the Marquis of Ailsa, asked him to come and stay for a while, which was a kindly gesture that he accepted gladly. After which he threw himself even more into his work, and it was from this time that he began to be more ostentatious and bizarre in his appearance.

*Unknown Italian Boy with bust of George IV,
Emma Soyer*

II

The Reforming Chef

The London Clubs, without which Surtees thought the social change brought about by the railways would have been incomplete, became more and more important during the first half of the nineteenth century, as meeting places for men of public affairs as well as country gentlemen from the Shires.

Most of the big clubs were founded at this time, where people with compatible social or political interests could meet easily, dine well and learn what was going on.

Three famous clubs – White's, Brooks's and Boodle's – all in St James's Street and still flourishing, were founded a century earlier, and were originally gaming clubs. But the new clubs, mostly founded in the 1830s and 1840s, were different. They were not just for the rich and idle; they were used by the new middle classes, and each had its own character. The Athenaeum catered for scholarship and the Church; members of the Travellers', next door in Pall Mall, had to show that at some time they had travelled five hundred miles from London; the Garrick was "to enable actors and men of education and refinement to meet on equal terms", and there were clubs for members of the armed services, and for those who had had careers or interests in India and the Far East. Nearly all these clubs were in St James's or Pall Mall – except the Garrick, over in Covent Garden – and this is still Clubland.

In 1837 a contemporary magazine listed twenty-five clubs in the area. About half survive today; some were founded later and may or may not still exist; others have amalgamated with clubs of similar interests, as have the University clubs. At this stage the clubs didn't have bedrooms as most do today, but were used by members as a town house, with dining-rooms, libraries and drawing-rooms, as well as gaming tables.

The Reform Act of 1832 widened the franchise, and with the general feeling of change and expansion in the air, so the clubs became more politically aligned.

Brooks's had always been a Whig stronghold, and in this Age of Reform was well placed. The Tories, however, felt a greater need to co-ordinate their ideas and, with the greater number of potential voters around, to present a strong opposition. Thus, the Duke of Wellington saw the need for a Tory Club, where members could meet easily and plan their strategy and, due largely to his efforts, the Carlton Club was founded, which became, as it is still, the bastion of the Tory Party.

It usually happens that the conserving party presents a more united front than the reforming party, which will always have its radicals, and this was true of the Whigs, who were known variously as Liberals and Radicals. The Radicals were a small but active group, eager for more change more quickly, and they began to feel the need for a club of their own, as they felt that Brooks's was not as aggressively political as they would have wished, or as the Carlton had become.

A small Reform Association was formed, meant to encourage people to register as voters, and to interest local political groups. This was not a success, though it did become a sort of dining club for a time. So more thought went into the best way to achieve their aims, and one of the leading figures in this was Edward Ellice (known as "Bear" Ellice because of his interests in the Hudson Bay Company). Some time later *The Times* wrote: "Edward Ellice's desire was to establish a club which should neither be exclusively Whig, like Brooks's, nor exclusively Radical ... one in which all those who professed to be Liberals might find a congenial home, and wherein social intercourse was to be considered as worthy of encouragement as purely party and political action. . . . Before calling the Reform Club into existence, Mr Ellice had appealed to Brooks's, of which he was a member, to widen its boundaries and embrace within them a large number of members belonging to all shades of Liberalism. At a meeting to consider his proposition it was decided by a large majority that the Club should continue limited in number and scope. After the vote had been taken Mr Ellice exclaimed, 'Well, gentlemen, we mean to start a club which will beat yours.' " And so, in the summer of 1837 the new Reform Club was born.

Both the Carlton and the Reform became so socially and politically influential that half a century later it was claimed that they were the two clubs in which English history was being made.

The Reform Club House, Pall Mall

The Reform was not as solidly Anglican as other clubs; there were many Nonconformists, many Roman Catholics, and Jews. Although ladies were not admitted as members until a few years ago, the Club was much more relaxed in allowing them to visit the premises and, on special occasions, to dine there. Talent was more important than birth – one well-known member, Joseph Paxton, of quite humble birth, had started his working life as a gardener. He later became famous as the gardener to the Duke of Devonshire, and designed the great conservatory at Chatsworth, but his great triumph was the Crystal Palace for the Great Exhibition of 1851, for which he was knighted.

It must have been very satisfying for Alexis Soyer, himself an innovator and reformer in his own field, to be appointed the first chef to the Club in 1837, when he was still in his twenties. This appointment turned out to be very important for him and helped to establish both his and the Club's reputation.

The Club building was designed by Sir Charles Barry, who, a few years earlier had designed the Travellers' Club next door. The two are in very different styles; the Reform is larger, with more self-confidence (Pevsner describes it as "maturity after lovable youth") and the interior has a large and impressive galleried hall.

The kitchens, which were to play so great a part in Soyer's future career, were designed in close collaboration and consultation between chef and architect. They became a show-place of the Club and Soyer loved to have visitors there and to show off all his new gadgets and machinery. They were reckoned to be the finest kitchens in London, and are minutely described and illustrated in Soyer's own *Gastronomic Regenerator*, as well as in contemporary magazines and newspapers. The well-known sectional drawing of the kitchens (with, of course, *le maître* in the centre) has been reproduced many times and is still sold by the Club.

One of his great innovations was to introduce gas cookers into his kitchen. This was a very new cooking fuel, though gas had been used for street lighting since quite early in the century. Pall Mall itself, where the Club stands, had been lit by gas since 1808, and the Gas, Light and Coke Company was registered by 1812. But it was not a cheap way of cooking; even when the greater flexibility and efficiency were taken into account it was still about twice the cost of coal. However, Soyer had to be in at the beginning of every new idea, and by 1841 the Reform Club was one of the first places to cook by gas.

Soyer was a great organiser and a great showman. But he was no good at writing. His artist wife, Emma, had had beautiful handwriting and had acted as his secretary, written all his letters and made out the menus. After her death Soyer, rather touchingly, took writing lessons to try to improve his own crabbed hand, but he didn't do well, perhaps because he was too busy doing other things to practise properly, and after a few months gave up the struggle.

He wasn't too busy, though, to show off the kitchens, even though he sometimes designated the task to an underling, if he thought the visitor wasn't important enough for his own attention; "It was curious to watch him, with his red velvet cap and spoon in hand, explaining to elegantly dressed ladies, and to the best blood of the aristocracy and nobility, his various methods of concocting soups of exquisite flavour, or his different styles of producing his dishes of fish, game, poultry, etc., at the same time giving full proof of his power over the art, by handing round either some properly made mulligatawny, or a basin of *sole à la maître d'hotel*, sending home the tasters positively rabid for their dinner, and wishing Soyer could be divided into as many pieces as a calf's head for his mock-turtle, that they might each have a bit of him in their cookery department. Sometimes he would suddenly plunge his finger, diamond ring and all, into what appeared to be a boiling

THE KITCHEN DEPARTMENT

appeared to be a boiling cauldron of glue, pass it across his tongue, wink his eye, and add either a little more salt, pepper, or some mysterious dust, known possibly only to to great artistes, to make it palatable. Then again, he would whisper chucklingly, 'I've a dish for Lord M—H——, for six o'clock, or a potage for Sir J. So-and-So at eight o'clock; let us taste it'.... Soyer, ambitious of glory, kept on producing new delicacies in return for every new manifestation of the delight with which his efforts were welcomed, and altogether created such a sensation among the members that ... political reform for the moment was absorbed in *les côtelettes à la reform,* and other equally new and delicious dishes which the wizard cook provided." These *côtelettes â la reform* (or *réforme*; he seemed to use both spellings) became his single best-known dish, now established in the *haute cuisine* repertory, and although at least one other club has

OF THE REFORM CLUB.

given its name to a dish – Boodle's Fool is a delicious orange confection – the dish of cutlets with Reform sauce is easily the most famous. I am delighted to learn that they are still on the menu at the Club, though the meat is now lamb instead of mutton.

The following recipe comes from Soyer's book *The Gastronomic Regenerator*:

Côtelettes de Mouton à la Reform

Chop a quarter of a pound of lean cooked ham very fine, and mix it with the same quantity of bread-crumbs, then have ten very nice côtelettes, lay them flat on your table, season lightly with pepper and salt, egg over with a paste-brush, and throw them into the ham and bread-crumbs, then beat them lightly with a knife, put ten spoonfuls of oil in a sauté-pan, place it over the fire, and when quite hot lay in the côtelettes, fry nearly ten minutes (over a moderate fire) of a light brown colour; to ascertain when done, press your knife upon the thick part, if quite done it will feel rather firm; possibly they may not all be done at one time, so take out those that are ready first and lay them on a cloth till the others are done; as they require to be cooked with the gravy in them, dress upon a thin border of mashed potatoes in a crown, with the bones pointing outwards, sauce over with a pint of the sauce reform, and serve. If for a large dinner you may possibly be obliged to cook the côtelettes half an hour before, in which case they must be very underdone, and laid in a clean sauté-pan, with two or three spoonfuls of thin glaze; keep them in the hot closet, moistening them occasionally with the glaze (with a paste-brush) until ready to serve; the same remark applies to every description of côtelettes.

So far so good, but the description of the sauce is more complicated, as it refers to three different kinds of sauce which have to be made first, though more probably in a big household or club, they would be ready in store as being 'foundation sauces'.

Sauce à la Reform

Cut up two middling-sized onions into thin slices and put them into a stewpan with sprigs of parsley, two of thyme, two bay-leaves, two ounces of lean uncooked ham, half a clove of garlic, half a blade of mace, and an ounce of fresh butter; stir them ten minutes over a sharp fire, then add two tablespoonfuls of Tarragon vinegar, and one of Chili vinegar, boil it one minute; then add a pint of brown sauce, or sauce Espagnole, three tablespoonfuls of preserved tomates [sic], and eight of consommé; place it over the fire until boiling, then put it at the corner, let it simmer ten minutes, skim it well, then place again over the fire, keeping it stirred, and reduce until it adheres to the back of the spoon; then add a good tablespoonful of red currant jelly, and half do. of chopped mushrooms; season a little more if required with pepper and salt; stir it until the jelly is melted, then pass it through a tammie into another stewpan. When ready to serve, make it hot, and add the white of a hard-boiled egg cut into strips half an inch long, and thick in proportion, four white blanched mushrooms, one gherkin, two green Indian pickles, and half an ounce of cooked ham, or tongue, all cut in strips like the white of egg; do not let it boil afterwards. This sauce must be poured over whatever it is served with.

A lot of work involved, and no handy tin of Cook-In sauce to help out either.

In *The Compleat Imbiber* no. 6 (1967) Ernest Atkinson wrote about Soyer and his mutton cutlets reform, and as well as the original receipt he had this version as given to him by the then chef at the Club:

Simplified receipt for Côtelettes à la Reform

Take your cutlets, season them lightly with pepper and salt, touch them over with flour and egg and breadcrumbs mixed with finely chopped ham, and chopped parsley. Cook them when the moment arrives in your sauté-pan, in oil.

Prepare also a reduction of vinegar, peppercorns and redcurrant jelly. Add to this demi-glace. Reduce and strain it.

Prepare a julienne of tongue, of ham cut very fine, of beetroot, of gherkins, and add this to your sauce.

Simmer all this in butter. Add the sauce described above. Add a knob of butter.

Let all these be ready at the moment your cutlets are done in your sauté-pan.

Put the sauce in a flat dish big enough to array the cutlets agreeably.

Lay them on top of the sauce. Add a noisette of butter to give a shine to them. Sprinkle over them strips of the white of boiled egg.

It was very fashionable in those days to name dishes after

important people or events, and there are other dishes *à la Reform* that Soyer created – he also gives a *Potage Marcus Hill*, named after the Club Chairman of the time. There is a dish of *Filet de Boeuf à la Réforme* and *Filets de Liévre, sauce Réforme*, which, apart from the meat itself does not differ greatly from the receipt for the Côtelettes as the sauce is the same in each case, but there is also a receipt for *Filets de Soles à la Réforme* which is somewhat different, and is as follows:

> . . . fillet two soles, beat each fillet flat; have ready a dozen oysters, blanched and chopped, which mix with four tablespoonfuls of forcemeat of whiting, and a little chopped eschalots; spread some on one fillet, then cover another over it, and so on till they are all done; put a little oil in a sauté-pan, with a little chopped eschalots, and a glass of white wine; lay your fillets in, season with a little pepper and salt, and put them in a moderate oven until tender; turn them over, and cut each into large diamonds, dress them round (points upwards) upon a dish, and put them in the hot closet; put ten tablespoonfuls of melted butter, and six do. [ditto] milk into the sauté-pan; place it over the fire, and when it boils pass it through a tammie; place it again over the fire, boil it a few minutes, add two pats of butter, and stir it till quite smooth; pour the sauce over the fillets, sprinkle some gherkins and ham (cut into strips half an inch long) over, and serve very hot.

The only things that this dish has in common with the others *à la Reform* seem to be the strips of gherkins and ham as a garnish. Ernest Atkinson then goes on to consider what wines would be suitable for drinking with such *à la Reform* dishes, and he suggests Beaujolais as his own choice, as he reckoned that such a variety of flavours would not be kind to a more delicate wine. But according to the then butler at the Club, with whom he discussed the matter, it would most likely have been a bourgeois claret, as according to old records the most popular wine was the club claret, usually a Cantenac from the Margaux regions of the Médoc.

It is quite true that Soyer gives little guidance as to what wines would be served as his splendid banquets, and the main references he makes himself are to champagne and cognac, though it is known that he kept a cupboard full of rare wines and liqueurs in his private room in the kitchens; presumably to offer to the many visitors he had to show round.

Part of the Reform Club Kitchen, enlarged

The kitchens have long since been modernised, and little of the original remains, but the Club still keeps the Soyer tradition going by having selected dishes made to his receipts on the menu reach day, and for special occasions, such as the Winterhalter Ball, to recreate some of his more elaborate concoctions and garnishes.

Although much of his time was given to preparing special dinners and banquets – one was given for the coronation of Queen Victoria at which hundreds were present – he was still aware that not everyone could, or would wish to, afford very grand meals, and there were always good, simple meals for Club members that were remarkably inexpensive and good value – and such is the tradition of much club cooking today. On one occasion Thackeray, seeing beans and bacon on the menu, cancelled a dinner date elsewhere, on the grounds that he had met an old friend who he hadn't seen for a long time.

Soyer was at the Reform for about a dozen years, and though on the whole it was a happy relationship, it was also quite often a stormy one. In 1843 he was insolent to one of the Committee members, soon to become Chairman, and a few months afterwards he wrote a letter to another member which became a matter for the Committee, who had "to consider the conduct of M. Soyer towards a certain member of the Club". Soyer had a severe ticking off, he apologised fully to the people concerned, and no further action was taken.

However, a little while later he was in trouble again, this time over financial matters. There had been some irregularity in the butcher's bill which had to be fully looked into, and it was by the narrowest majority that the Committee didn't dismiss him. He resigned though, while the investigation was going on, and some days later Lord Marcus Hill, the then Chairman, and usually a warm supporter of Soyer, ruled that "It appears that M. Soyer has been guilty of no dishonesty whatever but of great irregularity, and the Committee resolve that he be called in, reprimanded, and informed that a repetition of such conduct will be followed by immediate dismissal." But this was followed by a motion "that it is the opinion of this Committee that the charge against M. Soyer had not been substantiated, but that inasmuch as he has been guilty of great irregularity, his resignation is accepted." Other members of the staff were reprimanded as well, and, in the *Memoirs*, there is reference to Soyer always being ready and willing to help other servants of the club if they were in trouble, but "it has occurred that the very individuals who sought, at times, his good offices, were at other periods, untrue to him". Soyer may well have resented the staff who were called as witnesses against him, and thought that they had betrayed him.

Soyer was "daily in contact with scientific, literary, and artistic personages, whose company he courted, and would naturally give them some *recherchés petits soupers* in the Club, after the hours of business were over. The expenses were always shown with the vouchers, so that, with the exception of the knives and forks belonging to the Club, used on these occasions, the 'regenerator' felt that he was perfectly independent; on every attack made against him, he generally refuted it with so much good sense, vigour, and wit, that the members of the Committee mostly enjoyed with him a good laugh."

It seems that there was no good laugh about the butcher's bill, and it was most probably these little suppers that had caused the 'irregularity', but at the end of the month Soyer wrote to ask for his job back, and as nothing had actually been proved against him the Committee, by a majority of three, granted his reinstatement, and he remained at the Club for another six years. *Punch* reported this 'culinary intelligence' that M. Soyer was to stay at the Reform Club; "We happen to know that the increase of confidence has been immense, for a member who orders a chop no longer makes any observations as to how he would like it done, but leaves it

Lord Marcus Hill

entirely to the discretion of M. Soyer. We understand that the *chef de cuisine* is so extremely sensitive that he had been known to shed tears if a person ordering a basin of mutton broth has asked for the pepper, because the mere demand seems to throw a doubt on M. Soyer's powers of seasoning. At a recent house-dinner, a member of the committee held in his hand the resignation of M. Soyer, which was to have been peremptorily given in if a new arrangement of beef collops had been in the smallest degree objected to. By some this step may be regarded as unconstitutional; and it is probable that M. Soyer had in his remembrance the extreme step taken by EARL GREY to ensure the passing of the Reform Bill, when he caused it to be given out that he had in his pocket a *carte blanche* for the creation of Peers. The collops, however, on coming to a division, were perfectly successful, and their principle unanimously approved.

"We understand that M. Soyer has a few young gentlemen reading with him, as pupils, in his chambers; and that one of them, who is studying for the made-dish department, corresponding to what, in the legal profession, would be called the chancery, is likely to rise to culinary eminence. On the simple joint-side of the kitchen, or rather the common law of cookery, there is not so much scope for genius."

In May of 1846, with Committee disputes now far behind him, Soyer created what he termed "The most *recherché* dinner I ever dressed." This was for ten members of the Reform, the host being a Mr Sampayo. "The tradesmen received their orders a week previous to the dinner. The finest mullets I ever saw, as well as the Severn salmon were obtained at Grove's in Bond Street . . . At seven o'clock the live Severn salmon were brought to me, they having just arrived direct from Gloucester, and were boiled immediately, being just under ten minutes before the dinner, and placed upon the table, and were eaten in their greatest possible perfection. The finest of the poultry came from Bailey's, Davis Street, Grosvenor Square, and Townshends, Charles Street, Haymarket. The *foies gras* and some very fine fresh French truffles came from Morel's; the hors d'oeuvres from Hedge's and Butler's, Regent Street. The saddleback of lamb came from Newlands, Air Street, Piccadilly; the Welsh mutton from Slater's and the young green peas and a very expensive dessert came from Lewis Solomon's, Covent Garden. My being so minute in mentioning the names of the above tradespeople is not to advertise their fame . . . but merely to prove the trouble a real gourmet will take to furnish his table, Mr S— having called many times upon several of them himself, previous to his party taking place, to ascertain what his dinner was to be composed of."

The Welsh mutton appeared as *Côtelettes de Mouton Galloise à la Réform*, and as far as I know this is the first recorded mention of the dish on a menu.

The railway from Gloucester served him rather better than the boat from France, for there should have been another dish, of truffles stuffed with ortolans, which had been specially ordered from Paris. But the weather turned nasty, the boat was delayed, and the truffles, which had already been bought in London, had to be served simply *à l'essence de Madère*.

The ortolan is a very small bird much esteemed for its plumpness and flavour an, I believe it still is, in the Landes region of south-west France, where there is a great tradition of attracting all kinds of birds by using decoys, then netting them and fattening them up until they are reckoned right for eating. The ortolans, weighing about three ounces, were sometimes cooked on skewers, or stuffed with *foie gras*, or simply beheaded and cooked as they were with the insides (trail) left in. Sometimes they were cooked in truffles as Soyer had intended: he once said that "an ortolan can scarcely be truffled, but I will undertake that a truffle can be ortolaned" . . . but not, alas, on that occasion.

The Sampayo dinner was more or less a domestic affair for the Club members, but in July of the same year came the spectacular banquet given for the Egyptian ruler Ibrahim Pacha, on an official visit to London where he was received with great ceremony.

The banquet was given by over a hundred members of the Reform, headed by Lord Palmerston, then Foreign Secretary, and Admiral Sir Charles Napier. The account of this great feast was in every newspaper, reaching the French press too, and more space was given to the menu than to the speeches. The band of the Scots Fusilier Guards performed throughout the evening, and perhaps had to play harder and longer than usual to cover possible delays, as there seems to have been some disruption in the kitchen on this occasion, for, so the *Memoirs* tell us, there was "an unexpected display of insubordination on the part of his satellites". However Soyer, of course, threw himself into the breach. ". . . just when he was dressed to attend the princely recipient of the ovation, he was compelled to don his odd cap . . . and descending to the kitchen, soon set his 'aides' to the right about, and achieved his usual conquest." Very possibly he was showing off to such an extent that it was more than his hard-working 'satellites' could take.

Anyway, the Guards' band eventually played the guests into dinner with 'The Roast Beef of Old England', and the elaborate and extensive banquet began. All the recipes can be found in the *Gastronomic Regenerator*, but I cannot see any amateur cook trying them, as they are all heavily garnished with truffles, cocks' combs, lobster spawn and goodness knows what else.

It was usual to decorate important dishes, very fancifully, although Soyer wrote that he didn't like to go in for too much ornamentation. But as he put this at the beginning of his recipe for *Croustades of Bread for Removes*, which he fashioned into a breastplate (for a *Fillet of Beef à la Joan of Arc*) or a ship (for *Turkey à la Nelson*) I suppose ideas of ornamentation have to be relative. On this occasion the croustades were made into tiaras to display the *Quatres de Poulardes en Diadem* which, like the other two mentioned, are illustrated in the book. The high spot of the banquet was a specially created *Crême d'Egypte à l'Ibrahim Pacha*, which according to the *Sun* newspaper "was a pyramid about two feet and a half high, made of light meringue cake, in imitation of solid stones, surrounded with immense grapes and other fruit, but representing only the four angles of the pyramid through sheets of waved sugar, to show to the greatest advantage an elegant cream *à l'ananas*, on the top of which was resting a highly finished portrait of the illustrious stranger's father Mehemet Ali, carefully drawn on a round shape satin carton, the exact size of the top of the cream. The portrait was immediately observed by his Highness, who carefully took it up, and after showing it to several of his suite, placed it in his bosom. What was his Highness's astonishment, however, on again looking at the spot, to observe in the cream, as under glass, a highly finished portrait of himself surrounded by a carefully executed frame." The Pacha wanted to know how such portraits could be managed, and Soyer told him that they had been done from original

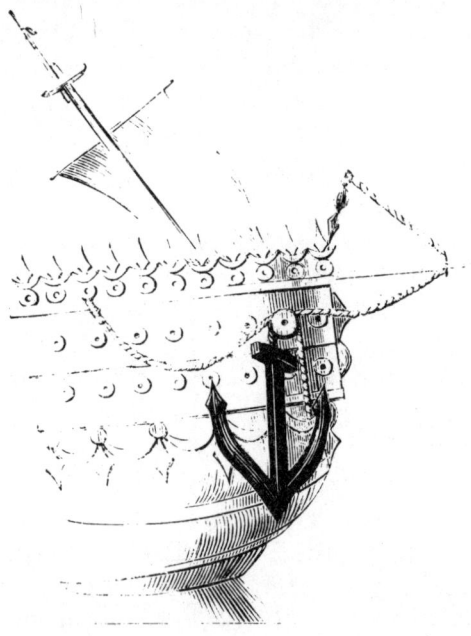

Turkey à la Nelson

sketches, and the portrait on cream was "drawn on wafer paper which being placed on the damp jelly, representing the glass, dissolves, and nothing remains of the wafer paper but the appearance of the portrait painted in light water colours. The imitation of the gilt frame is made with the *eau-de-vie* of Danzig and gold water mixed with the jelly, the gold leaf of which forms the frame." The dish was slid round the table so that everyone could see it, but although the surrounding fruit was eaten, no one was bold enough to tackle the meringue cake which went away untouched.

It was a rather more elegant dinner for the 'illustrious stranger' than the one he had had to put up with the day before, when again according to the *Sun*, he had taken a river trip to Gravesend. The journey took longer than had been expected, and there was no food available until his

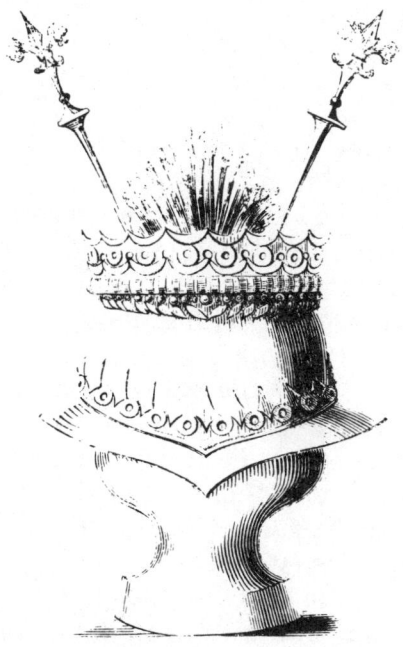

Croustade à la Jeanne d'Arc

party scoured the town to find "a joint of beef from one place, a ham from another, and a goodly supply of champagne from a third", and this 'hasty meal' had to be laid out on a tablecloth on the deck. It is a pity that Soyer wasn't of the party, so that he could (and surely would) have demonstrated his Magic Stove.

It was during this visit to London that Palmerston

wrote to the Queen that "Ibrahim Pacha learnt to write his name while your Majesty's messenger was waiting with your Majesty's album; and that when he had written his name in the book he threw away the pen, saying that as the first time in his life that he had written his name had been for the Queen of England, so it should also be the last, for he would not write it again for anybody else. . . ." I suppose that means he wrote it in English characters for the first time, as I feel sure he must have been able to do so in his native language.

Soyer eventually resigned from the Club in 1850, and his reasons for doing so are not immediately clear. Probably there were several contributory factors, though the one given in the *Memoirs* – that club members were to be allowed to bring in more guests for meals, and Soyer thought that this would make the place too much like a restaurant – seems the least likely. For someone of his personality and his skills, the thought of being able to provide for more people, among them many eminent ones, would, I believe, have pleased rather than discouraged him. But there was also the suggestion that he might not have been able to have so many pupils or 'improvers' in his kitchen, which must have been a profitable business for him; the Club Committee had been critical of him from time to time, and he never took kindly to criticism; and there had been at least two suggestions (with offers of financial support) that he should open a restaurant of his own and the Great Exhibition planned for the following year, offered new opportunities for his talents. Also, he had been at the Reform for a good many years, and perhaps just felt the need for change.

When his decision was announced, *Punch* one again weighed in with its usual brand of mock solemnity and terrible puns: "Considerable excitement has, for some time past, been occasioned at the West End, by the rumour of its being the intention of Mons. SOYER to resign his position as *Chef* of the Reform Club. A few days ago the melancholy rumour was changed into frantic certainty, and it became generally known that SOYER had resigned the basting spoon of office, into the hands of the Committee, and had put his spit at their feet. On the first announcement of this intelligence, the enquiries were general, whether Lord JOHN [Russell], then Prime Minister, would go out with SOYER, whose retirement, it was said, had shaken the cabinet to atoms, but on inquiry, it was ascertained that the cabinet shaken to atoms, was a cabinet pudding, which was being prepared at the moment, when in a state of pitiable agitation the *Chef* resolved on throwing up the office he has so long adorned.

"Various causes have been assigned for the step that has been taken, but nothing is positively known. By some it is intimated that there has long been a coolness over the kitchen fire, and that SOYER has vacated his office, in the hope of finding a much wider range for his abilities. Some insinuate that he was dissatisfied with his subordinates, and that on seeing a sirloin of beef going round on the spit with improper velocity, he expressed his horror at things taking such a turn.

"In some quarters it is whispered that there are certain provisions contained in a bill which the *Chef* thought necessary to the maintenance of his government; but those provisions requiring a bill of enormous magnitude, were objected to in committee as extravagant, and not in accordance, with the moderate tastes of the members, but SOYER declared it impossible to carry on the culinary government on a paltry scale of economy. Many of his plans required very early peas, but he and the Committee having, it is said, split upon these peas, and the latter refusing to shell out, the *Chef* had no alternative. Others, give out with an air of some authority, that SOYER's schemes were so gigantic, as to require a supply of five hundred new stewpans; but the requisition having been characterised by an 'exquisite' belonging to the Committee as something '*really stew-pan-dous*', the pride of the *Chef* was

Affecting scene, Soyer resigning the Great Stewpan

offended, and he resolved at once on retirement. This affair will cause much embarrassment, as it will require the filling up of several offices which the genius of SOYER was enabled to combine. There must be a minister for foreign affairs, including all the French dishes, and none but a successor of the PRESIDENT DU PATY could hope to preside over the pies. As to the puffs, the loss of SOYER will not be so severely felt, as most of the puffs he was so famous for manufacturing were for his own use."

In spite of earlier difficulties with the committee, when he did leave it was on very amicable terms, and Lord Marcus Hill the Chairman and members such as Thackeray (who as 'Gobemouche' may have been responsible for some of the *Punch* anecdotes) and George Augustus Sala, remained his good friends. Sala was responsible for the design of Soyer's Symposium at the 1851 Exhibition, but before coming to that let us look at some of the other ways in which Soyer spent his time.

III
A Broth of A Boy

Soyer made his name through his association with the Reform Club and his aristocratic patrons. However, he was never concerned with this kind of cooking alone, and was always eager to help those who were less well off. Perhaps there was an element of self-advertisement in this, he was never 'backward in coming forward', but he was warm-hearted and generous, and genuinely concerned for others, and, perhaps due to a frugal French upbringing, felt upset at the thought of people not making the best of the food that they had available.

In 1845 there was a bad corn harvest in England which affected the price and availability of bread, and in the same year the potato crop failed in Ireland, which was even more serious as the country depended to a very great extent on this as staple food, and to make matters worse, the crop failed again the following year.

The Corn Laws were repealed in this country, which although that meant the price of bread didn't rise, it didn't fall either, and many people reached starvation level.

Early in 1847 Soyer started a long correspondence in *The Times* – he was a great one for letters to *The Times*, which they printed at length, giving them the space and prominence that would be impossible today – to raise public subscriptions for soup kitchens both in London and Dublin, and started the ball rolling himself with a donation of £30.

Soup kitchens were quite common in those days of Victorian benevolence, and soup and blankets for the poor were expected from the better-off middle classes as part of their new responsibilities, and it must have been about this time that the nanny-phrase of "many a poor boy would be glad of that" was so frequently used as some unfortunate child was made to sit over his congealing rice-pudding.

A soup kitchen soon started in Leicester Square, supplying about forty gallons of soup a day to more than two hundred people, and Soyer made plans for bigger and better kitchens, and invented a soup boiler to make it possible to feed thousands rather than hundreds.

The correspondence in *The Times* continued, and he published some of his recipes for soup, saying that his "devotion to this important cause being to take every possible advantage of every kind of nutritious substances, animal and vegetable, and fish, and to convert them, by study and judgement, into a wholesome and cheap aliment for the millions."

The first recipe for his soup doesn't sound very appetising for us today, but was cheap to produce and must have been welcome as a source of nourishment to the poor and hungry.

The Recipe for Soup no. 1

I first put one ounce of dripping into a saucepan (capable of holding two gallons of water), with a quarter of a pound of leg of beef without bones, cut into square pieces about half an inch, and two middle-sized onions, peeled and sliced. I then set the saucepan over a coal fire, and stirred the contents round for a few minutes with a wooden (or iron) spoon until fried lightly brown. I had then ready washed the peeling of two turnips, fifteen green leaves or tops of celery, and the green part of two leeks (the whole of which, I must observe, are always thrown away). Having cut the above vegetables into small pieces I threw them into the saucepan with the other ingredients, stirring them occasionally over the fire for another ten minutes; then added half a pound of common flour (any farinaceous substance would do), and half a pound of pearl barley, mixing it all well together. I then added two gallons of water, seasoned with three ounces of salt, and a quarter of an ounce of brown sugar, stirred occasionally until boiling, and allowed it to simmer very gently for three hours, at the end of which time I found the barley perfectly tender. The above soup has been tasted by numerous noblemen, members of Parliament, and several ladies, who have lately visited my kitchen department, and who have considered it very good and nourishing.

The cost, at full price, is as follows:

Quarter of a pound of leg of beef at 4d per lb	1d
Two ounces of dripping-fat, at 4d per	½d
Two onions and other vegetables	1d
Half a pound of flour, second, at 1½d per lb	¾d
Half a pound of pearl barley, at 3d per lb	½d
Three ounces of salt with half an ounce of brown sugar	¼d
Fuel	1d
Two gallons of water	0d
	6d

This soup will keep several days, when made as above described. The above expense make it come to ¾d per quart in London; but as almost everything can be had at much less cost in the country, the price of this soup will be still more reduced. In that case a little additional meat might be used; and by giving away a small portion of bread or biscuit, better support would be given to the poor at a trifling cost, and no one, it is to be hoped, hereafter, would hear of the dreadful calamity of starvation.

Carting away the dead at Skibbereen, Irish Famine

This was followed in the same letter by another recipe, similar but even cheaper and quicker to make, and then followed instructions for making 100 gallons (which was stirred by a piece of board the shape and size of a cricket bat), and he gives careful orders about the way the vegetables should be sliced, always on the slant "which facilitates greatly the cooking."

All this produced further letters in *The Times*, some correspondents praising his ingenuity and philanthropy, others complaining that this would not produce "soup for the poor" but "poor soup", and one housewife, signing herself 'Poor Cook' complained that his figures were wrong, and the cost was three halfpence a quart, not three-farthings as Soyer had said.

One story that appears in the *Memoirs* is of a friend of Soyer who, when reading of his recipes, came running into the Reform Club, "hat in hand, with glowing face, and so exhausted that it was some seconds before he could articulate. Meanwhile M. Soyer, always ready for a joke, said to his friend, 'Well, old boy, I hope this time I am not to be disappointed; the last one was a girl, and, as I intend standing godfather to the next, I trust you have come to inform me that it is a son and heir.' In answer to this interesting inquiry, the reply was, 'dripping's up!' 'What–' replied Soyer. 'My dear fellow,' continued Mr W.....r, 'if you had told me that you intended publishing your receipts, I could have gone into the market, and bought tons of dripping; and we might between us have pocketed a few hundred!' Poor Soyer, whose mind was never troubled about the state of the market, as to its rising or falling, fell back on his sofa in a fit of laughter... This gentleman afterwards accompanied M. Soyer on his governmental mission to Ireland, and did good service."

Punch delighted in anecdotes about Soyer, and when in the spring of 1847, the government asked Soyer to go out to Dublin to use his ideas there, the paper nicknamed him "A broth of a boy", and depicted an Irishman saying, "The soup is delicious – for the more I take of it the more it brings the water into my mouth." Much of the sneers about the soup must have been made from jealousy of some of his colleagues, and perhaps also, a resentment at Soyer's own style of self-advertisement, but anyway, off he went to Dublin, and although the nutritious value of his soups was questioned by some, the *Lancet* pronounced that there was nothing wrong with the soup, but that more solid food was essential to keeping a working man going through the day.

Not an easy thing to do given the conditions prevailing in poor famine-wracked Ireland at the time.

The Government was particularly interested in his plans for the new type of model soup kitchen that Soyer had invented, and he was given time off from the Reform Club to go to Dublin, and a new kitchen was built in the grounds of the Royal Barracks there.

He describes this in the book the *Poor Man's Regenerator*, published soon after his return, and it demonstrates his ingenuity in kitchen planning and layout.

The kitchen was a temporary structure of boards and canvas measuring about 40'x48'. Inside there was a steam boiler on wheels, which could contain three hundred gallons, with at one end an oven heated by the same fire, which was in "an excavation to contain coals", and the oven was capable of taking a hundred-weight of bread.

Round the outside of the boiler were eight *bain-maries*, holding 1,000 gallons; cutting tables for the vegetables and meat were at the two ends, with tubs on wheels for soaking the vegetables, and chopping blocks for meat stored underneath. There were storage boxes for condiments hung round the roof supports, and water-butts and storage tubs were clustered round these supports as well.

At one end of the building was a row of tables with holes let in to take the enamelled quart-sized basins, with metal spoons chained to them. Other tables had bowls of water and sponges for cleaning out the soup bowls.

The soup took about an hour to make, if flour or oatmeal were used as the thickeners, rather longer if corn meal or dried peas were used, then when it was ready it was kept in the *bain-maries* until ladled into the basins as the recipients

M. Soyer's model soup kitchen

were admitted. Outside the tent was a zigzag passage where a hundred people stood waiting for admission. The reason he gives for this was "in order to prevent the crowding together of the poor, which causes the propagation of infectious diseases," but remembering his delight in having his clothes, visiting cards and so on *à la zougzoug*, this design may have been something of a trade-mark as well.

A bell was rung when the soup was ready and the people filed in, grace was said and they were given "sufficient time" to eat their quart of soup before cleaning their basins and going out of the kitchen at the opposite end to enable the next lot to come in. The "sufficient time" was six minutes, and a thousand could be fed in an hour.

Kitchen for soup or for the Army

Some people were given soup to take home if they had tickets, given out by charitable organisations, or the money to pay, and there was a meals-on-wheels distribution scheme of ingeniously designed horse-drawn carts which had fires underneath so the food stayed hot.

Soyer was justifiably proud of his inventions and goes on to suggest that such boilers would be a great service to the army – a forecast of his future activities.

There was so much demand for his recipes that Soyer wrote his little book, the *Poor Man's Regenerator, or Charitable Cookery*, which sold for sixpence, and for every copy sold he donated one penny to charity in a typically generous gesture.

When he came back to London he took up the cause of the

poor silk weavers of Spitalfields, who although their trade had once been very profitable, had fallen on bad times, and the demand for their work had declined largely due to the importing of cheap foreign goods. In 1839, according to Mayhew, the output of the Spitalfields workers accounted for about one-tenth of all the silk goods produced in Great Britain, and the average earnings of a skilled weaver would have been about 15s a week. Within ten years, this had dropped to about 5s weekly and many were unemployed.

There had been an Act of Parliament forbidding the importing of foreign silk goods, but this was repealed in 1826 and higher duties imposed instead. However, later on a commercial treaty with France allowed cheaper imported silks into the country, with the consequent decline in demand for home produced work.

Many of the silk weavers were Huguenots and worked very hard, not only at their trade but also in making their neighbourhood as pleasant as possible. Mayhew records that at the beginning of the century there was a "Floricultural Society, an Historical Society, and a Mathematical Society, all maintained by the operative silk-weavers." They bred singing birds, and "they passed their leisure hours, and generally the whole family dined on Sundays, at the little gardens in the environs of London, now mostly built upon."

The houses in the neighbourhood were built very much to a standard pattern with two rooms downstairs, and the workroom above with large windows, known as 'long lights' stretching the whole length of the room to enable as much light as possible to enter. With the decline in demand, and the rise of the middle-man or factor, who took his profit first, conditions for the weavers became very poor indeed. The children were sick, and often the parents could not afford to send them to school, except to Sunday school, and the parents had to work for fifteen hours a day to earn anything at all. There is an account of one man, working on silk for umbrellas, who used to get 1s a yard for it which had later been reduced to 10d, and he didn't know if he would get even that next time. "Weavers were all a-getting poorer, and masters all a-getting country houses. His master had been a-losing terrible, he said, and yet he'd just taken a country mansion." He got 10d a yard for the silk that would later sell at a guinea. "What would sixpence extra on that be to the purchaser, and yet that extra sixpence would be three or four shillings a week to him, and go a long way towards the rent?" Food was scarce and poor; he went on to say that the family had 4 lb of leg of beef for the week, and 3 lb flank on Sunday, "lucky to get that, too, eh?" between a family of six. "Now, I should like a piece of roast beef, with the potatoes done under it, but I shall never taste that again. And yet . . . that there sixpence on this umbrella would just do it. But what's that to people! What's it to them if we starve? . . . What's to become of us all – nine thousand of us here – besides wives and children – I can't say."

Because they were hard workers, and skilled at their trade, there was a good deal of public sympathy for the weavers and some efforts made to help them, largely by the well-tried formula of charitable soup kitchens, many of which were set up by the Huguenots and the Quakers in the neighbourhood.

Soyer wrote another of his long letters to *The Times*, and described a visit he had made to one of the weavers at home, where the children had eaten nothing for twenty-four hours, and then it had been only half-rotten apples and pieces of bread that had been given to their father, and "the only piece of furniture in that gloomy abode of misery was the weaving-machine, now at rest, and which in time of prosperity, was used to provide food, and made, if not a wealthy, at least a happy home of those now wretched and destitute families, and the scientific production of which has often, and even now, adorns the persons of thousands of the aristocracy and gentry of the country," and he goes on to hope that wearers of these luxuries will not forget their fellow creatures in distress. There is an extract from the *Satirist* at the time that comments in much the same way that "A public breakfast and *fête* was this week given in aid of the distressed needlewomen at Stockwell. Perhaps if, instead of this mockery, the Lord Mayor, who presides, and Alderman Farebrother who *lent* his villa for the occasion, had inquired how many poor needleworkers partook of a private meal that same day, their philanthropy would have been more apparent. But Mayors and Aldermen never feel more inclined to guzzle than in their moments of philanthropic weakness."

There *was* an attempt to do something, and Soyer established one of his model kitchens in the church of St Matthias with the help and support of the vicar. "M. Soyer has erected a soup kitchen in one of the most densely populated parts of Spitalfields, from which excellent peas panada and meat soup are distributed to the destitute in quantities amply sufficient for a hearty meal at the cost of only one penny! Many hundreds are daily relieved at the kitchen, while the remainder of the soup and bread is daily given away to many poor families in the neighbourhood whose exigencies are more

A weaver's room in Spitalfields

pressing and demand additional relief. Subscriptions for the support of so meritorious an undertaking are of course necessary, and it is to be hoped that the claims of the industrious weavers of Spitalfields on the sympathies of their countrymen will not be overlooked." Thus *The Times* weighed in, but there were so many demands for donations to every kind of charity and the parish itself had very few wealthy inhabitants among its ten thousand parishioners, that it was difficult to get enough money to keep the kitchen going, and Soyer's appeals for subscriptions didn't produce very much.

He was not at a loss for ideas for very long, and in order to boost funds he arranged an exhibition of Emma's paintings at the Prince of Wales' Bazaar in Regent Street under the name of 'Soyer's Philanthropic Gallery'. The exhibition was well received and the pictures admired. "There is a sort of comfortable sensation in the saloon, as if the walls were peopled by lively, good humoured personages. The staircase which the visitor has to ascend, is adorned with flower-pots on each side, to add to the general effect, and even the card of admission, fancifully painted, and cut into a rhomboid form [Soyer *à la zougzoug* again], shows the determination of the tasteful exhibitor to do something out of the beaten track." However tasteful the exhibition might be it didn't produce a great deal of money, and although the total of £259.11s meant that another fifty thousand rations could be distributed, it couldn't keep the kitchen going. However it did produce an 'Ode to M. Soyer', part of which went:

> *Yet, Soyer! great as was thy fame*
> *New glories now adorn this name;*
> *For, though the rich thy art did claim,*
>   *Thou heard'st the poor man's cry:*
> *When famine scourged green Erin's land,*
> *Thy generous heart swift succour plan'd*
> *And from thy able, willing hand,*
>   *Was poured a rich supply.*

> *I almost fancy that* her [Emma] *eyes,*
> *Who left thee for her native skies,*
> *Looked from her home, in Paradise,*
>   *Upon thy work – and smiled!*
> *For angel hearts rejoice to see*
> *The plants of human charity!*
> *Without whose fruits this world would be*
>   *A drear and gloomy wild.*

Soyer certainly was not averse to publicity and praise for his efforts, but he did practise what he preached and set out to provide the poor with as good a diet as possible given the small means at their disposal. And he deplored waste.

In the introduction to his *Charitable Cookery* he entreats that care should be taken "that nothing is wasted in the way of food, either individually or collectively, in any family in the kingdom."

When he published the soup recipes he wrote, "I did not suppose that they would meet with the entire approbation of the nation, particularly by those who imagine that nothing can be good except plenty of animal food is used for the subsistence of man . . . As regards the peelings and ends of vegetables which is used in my receipts, it is a well-known fact, that the exterior of every vegetable, roots in particular, contain more flavour than the interior of it; which is my reason for recommending only the washing well of those vegetables before they are cut for use, thereby increasing the vegetable produce of the country, and using that which has hitherto only increased the *malaria* of our courts and alleys by its decomposition."

Very sensible advice, rather in advance of his time, and at one stroke not only improving the diet of the poor, but helping to clear up litter as well.

Most of the recipes in the *Charitable Cookery* are for basic soup, none of which I think we would wish for today, though there are one or two others, such as the fish curry that could be adapted to modern taste, but his ideas of economy and frugality were much in tune with the Victorian values of the middle classes, and this theme was continued in his later, and more interesting, books.

Soyer was already well known for the way in which he had organised the kitchens at the Reform Club, as well as his kitchens for the provision of soup to the Irish poor, and in 1847 he was asked to design yet another kitchen, this time for a steam-vessel, the *Guadalquiver,* owned by a Mr Harbottle, a cigar merchant, who needed a boat to carry goods and passengers to Cuba and round the island. The boat was built at Liverpool and Soyer designed and planned the work with the firm of Bramah and Tristige of Piccadilly who made this "Compact and commodious kitchen" before the *Guadalquiver* "left Liverpool for the Spanish Main . . . like all similar contrivances by M. Soyer, the present one combines great economy of space with the most methodical arrangement; since it affords every possible convenience for cooking large dinners if required, and without confusion, in the small space of eight feet by seventeen feet long." The *Illustrated London News* gave a detailed drawing and explanation of this kitchen which is really remarkably compact and well planned. I was once told by an architect that today the actual working space used in a kitchen, regardless of the overall size of the room, is seven foot by fourteen, so Soyer's measurements of eight by seventeen must have been about right, considering the more cumbersome appliances of the time. Some of the designers of present day kitchens in small flats might do worse than consider some of his ideas. His designs have well outlasted the *Guadalquiver* which was wrecked within two years.

There was one kitchen though, that he designed on paper only. That was his 'Kitchen at Home' which he wrote about at length in the *Gastronomic Regenerator,* his first book of importance, in which he not only describes the large kitchens of the Reform Club but gives detailed drawings of My Kitchen at Home, the Bachelor's Kitchen and the Cottage Kitchen – "my intention, in giving the plans of several smaller kitchens, is to prove what I have before advanced, that I could easily introduce any of my plans or apparatus, into kitchens of the smallest dimensions." He goes on to give recipes more suitable for the smaller household than those contained in the main body of the book, including a menu for a dinner party at home, which, although far more than anyone would have at home these days, is nearer to present day tastes than one written at the same time, for a dinner for ten people that he cooked at the Reform Club.

This "Kitchen at Home" caused him some embarrassment at one time, for although he had intended to build it and have it on show for anyone interested to come and look, he never got round to doing so. At the time he was living with M. Simonau, the artist through whom he had met Emma, and who had married Emma's mother. The two widowers lived modestly near Leicester Square, and one lady who had read about the kitchen and wanted to see it, called on M. Simonau with the excuse that she wanted to have her portrait painted. Once she had been admitted to the apartments she had a good look round, and although she expected to see plenty of pictures on the walls hadn't expected the muddle that greeted her: "The room of the artist was a mixture of everything – works of art, old china, bronzes, old furniture, pictures and drawings; besides, the bed was not made up, a feather bed and mattress lying on the floor, and on a beautiful drawing-room table lay carrots, onions, leeks, and cabbages, *pêle-mêle* with the scrag of mutton the servant was getting ready, but which she did not dare to cook."

Simonau made an appointment for her to return the following week for her portrait sitting, then went off to "attend to a little culinary business" in the next room where she followed him and saw even more confusion. The lady asked if he was expecting Soyer to dine with him and Simonau replied that he did not always do so, but as Mademoiselle Cerito was expected that afternoon for her sitting, Soyer would probably be there too, as he was a great admirer of that dancer. At that point Soyer did come in and the lady asked to see his famous Kitchen at Home. Soyer wasn't often at a loss for words so

Soyer's miniature kitchen, and moveable balance grating

managed to get out of it by saying that "My kitchen at home *is out of town*, and, as I am unfortunately a bachelor, I do not see a chance of granting your request," and Simonau, picking up his cue, said "*Sacresti*, madame, I forgot to tell you we had a country-box." So the lady was thwarted, although she had her portrait painted and became a frequent visitor to the Reform Club, but had to be content with seeing the kitchens there.

IV

Soyer at Large

Some of the most endearing – and often maddening – characteristics of Alexis Soyer were his immense energy, enthusiasm, love of pleasure and enjoyment. He was quick-witted and full of jokes and fun. But he always took his work very seriously and never stopped thinking up new ideas, inventions, designs, ways of making things different and interesting. One well known story about him is his answer to Lord Melbourne's question when he visited Soyer in the Reform Club kitchens: "How is it you have such a number of pretty female assistants?" "My Lord," was the reply, "we do not want plain cooks here."

He was an original, and excited interest in everything he did. He was generous with his money, and would subscribe to any good cause that he was asked for, and once at least was badly caught by his own generosity when he fell in with a fellow-countryman called Phillippe, who was a conjurer – and a gambler. He persuaded Soyer to invest heavily in railway shares, which turned out badly. Even worse, Phillippe disappeared leaving Soyer to settle the debts of more than a thousand pounds. It is typical of Soyer's good nature, and also his naivety in such business matters, that he wrote to Phillippe thus: "My Dear and Good Phillippe, – You are a naughty fellow. You came to see me, not finding me at home, you ought to have written; but believe me, my good friend, notwithstanding the misfortune weighing heavily upon us – more particularly upon me, because I never had a wish to speculate in anything, being satisfied with the produce of my humble talent... I hope, however, that we shall have to live and love each other for a long time to come on this earth... London is full of people, and Christmas will put us on our legs again."

He loved the stage and all theatrical entertainments, especially ballet. He would go often to see whatever play took his fancy and, although he vowed he would never marry again, he had a great fondness for the ballerina Fanny Cerito, and would go to see her perform whenever he could, dedicated various of his dishes to her and wrote a ballet for her called 'La Fille de l'Orage'. The ballet was full of transformation scenes, and 'effects' with storms, lightning, flames, and passion between goddess and mortal, – and was impossible to perform. However, all these attentions came to nothing, and Fanny later married a violinist called St Leon.

Of course, in those days it was necessary to dress formally for the theatre, and Soyer would easily turn himself from chef

A London theatre, c. 1840

to man-about-town, and even then he had to have his little joke, once arriving at Her Majesty's Theatre in morning dress, whereupon the commissionaire was about to turn him away for not being properly dressed, but looked again and saw Soyer now in full evening dress, having contrived a trick suit that converted from one style to the other when he pulled a string.

He knew everybody, and was always at the heart of any party, and after the theatres there was always supper in one of the popular eating places, one favourite being Frost's in Bow Street, where there were always friends to join him at supper. On one occasion one of his friends had bought a pair of fowls to take home but Soyer decided otherwise, and while others kept this particular friend occupied, he took the birds into the kitchen and made a fricassée. He returned to the group, and suggested supper, but the owner of the birds refused, saying that he had already been to Jacquets, – a popular *à la mode* house of the time on the east side of Drury Lane – but was persuaded to stay, and in the end ten of them had a good supper of fricassée of chicken. The poor man – his name has not been revealed – was so delighted with the food that he ordered brandy all round, and it was only later when he was about to go home that he realised that the birds were missing and that he had not only lost his next day's supper but had paid out for the brandy, which cost him 2s 6d. "As to Soyer, he positively screamed, and in the heat of his delight, going homewards, upset several of his friends in the snow." One has to assume he forgave Soyer as most people did, but the occasion was one when the schoolboy humour must have tried his friends very much.

If he didn't go to supper at such places it was quite likely that, elegantly dressed as he would have been after the theatre, he would "quietly and slyly often dive into some obscure place and purchase two-pennyworth of fried fish! eating it with the greatest relish as he walked along."

His acquaintanceship with so many of the theatrical world brought him a commission, soon after he left the Reform Club, that must have given him great pleasure. This was suggested by Mr Lumley the director of Her Majesty's Theatre who wanted to have a *fête champêtre* to honour Monsieur Scribe and Monsieur Halevy the two famous French dramatists.

This was originally to be for 500 people, but in the end about 2000 took part. It was an enormous success with dishes created in honour of the two Frenchmen, the most spectacular of which was called the *Croustade Shakespearienne à la Halevy-Scribe* which was a model, made of cake, of the ship in the Tempest, with *chartreuses des pêches*, in imitation of barrels for cargo, and, framed in jelly, the portraits of the two visitors. There were waves of spun sugar, and jelly with grapes, apricots and other fruits embedded inside to represent the wrecked cargo round the ship. *Punch* was enthusiastic about the whole affair and paid tribute to Soyer's ingenuity: "Alexis Soyer – How I admire you! You appear to me to be the only man of our time who has adequately comprehended the mission of the cook. In your hands the *casserole* becomes eloquent, and the *marmiton* utters its moral. Shakespeare tells us of the 'tongues in trees, books in the running brooks, Sermons in stones;' and shall the dinner-table be mute? – shall there be no voice in a *pièce de résistance*, no revelation in a *relevé substantiel*? You have seized this want, and in your hands every *plat* has its point, every *entremet* its epigram."

Another of his jokey dishes, though this time not at the expense of a friend's supper, was his 'aerial dish'. It was planned that six well-known chefs should each produce something new, the challenge being to produce the "newest, lightest and most delicate dish!", and the judges were not to know who had made which dish until the end.

All this took place at an hotel in Slough where the six judges and the six chefs sat down at the table, had their soup and fish, then were presented with five of the competing dishes, all of which were considered good. But where was the sixth? With real showman's skill the dish named *'La Croustade Sylphe en surprise à la Cerito* was brought in, and when the lid of the dish was lifted, out flew a pigeon that immediately took

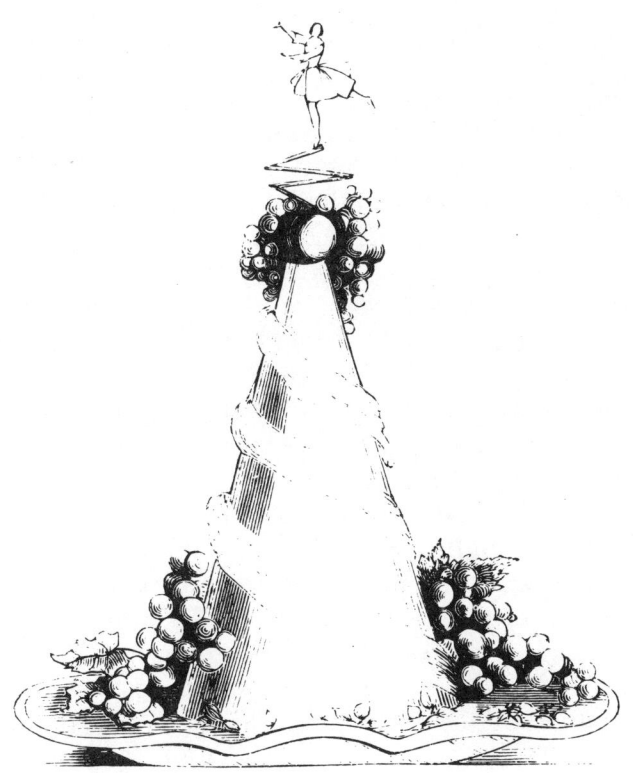

Lucille Graun and Cerito's Sultane Sylphe à la Fille de l'Orage

off for London. However, the showman and the chef always combined in Soyer, and the dish was revealed to have a false bottom, and the judges were then given a salad of grouse fillets, and in another part of the dish "artificial côtelettes and mushrooms were sweetly resting on a *crême aux pêches*". The cutlets and mushrooms were presumably made of cake or marzipan or some such, and although the story doesn't specify the winner of the competition we can guess who it was.

Soyer had made a bet, a few days before, that he would send part of his dish from Slough to London in a way that was faster than anything except the electric telegraph, and, as soon as the dish appeared, the friends in London with whom he had made the bet were telegraphed that the dish was on its way, and fourteen minutes later the pigeon appeared, with a note asking for the wager payment of £50 to be made to Soyer. *Punch* was always ready to have an affectionate dig at Soyer – Thackeray was a regular contributor and admired and respected Soyer a great deal, but was also able to see him as an often rather ridiculous figure and a show-off, though there was never anything malicious in what he wrote.

The following extract from *Punch* is typical of such comments: "Early last week, M. Soyer – warm from the Reform Club kitchen – was enjoying his skate in St James's Park. Having laid out an imaginary dinner for a hundred upon the ice, he boldly skated to the thinnest place, and went souse into the water. Many persons believed the immersion of the cook to be the effect of accident. By no means: with that enthusiasm that marks and heightens the character of the man, M. Soyer spontaneously went through the ice that he might arrive at the full knowledge of the use and abuse of – dripping."

The version of the same incident given in the *Memoirs* is also typical – "In the course of this year an accident occurred to Soyer, which might have ended fatally. While skating in St James's Park, the ice suddenly broke under him, and the *chef* was immersed; fortunately, assistance was near at hand, and he was soon extricated, and taken to the Society's reception-tent, where every attention was paid him, until he was himself again. Soyer gratefully handed over to the Royal Humane Society the sum of ten guineas, and was made a life-governor.

"This incident set Soyer immediately to work in a new direction; and, ever intent upon his one great object, that of accelerating the march of civilization, he forwarded to the Society a novel method of saving life during the skating season, which met with general approval, and received the Society's thanks."

We are not told of the life-saving method or if it was ever put to use.

On one occasion he was invited by the chef to Windsor Castle for a birthday dinner, and Soyer went along accompanied by an old friend, as he disliked travelling alone. The friend, nicknamed 'Briolet' was clearly a soul-mate of Soyer, as he is described as being "full of life, puns, comic songs, slang Parisian talk, and who could dance admirably." When they were walking from the coach to their chef friend's house it began to rain heavily, and Briolet opened Soyer's umbrella that had been carefully wrapped up, and they discovered that it had a huge hole in it, more than a foot round. They still put up the umbrella and walked through the Windsor streets chatting away as if they were quite unaware of anything unusual, much to the mirth of the good people of the town. When they reached their friend's they affected astonishment at finding the umbrella in such a condition and claimed that they knew nothing about it. Of course they may not have realised the hole was there until they opened it up, but afterwards they obviously made the best joke they could out of it.

SOYER never remarried after Emma died and their child died with her, so it was with mixed feelings, mainly surprise and pleasure, that in 1851 he got a letter from Paris, signed Alexis Lamain who claimed to be his son. The letter explained how the young Lamain had been brought up by his mother, and, after she had died, by an old friend until *he* died when his mother's brother took care of him. He had always wanted to know who his father was and eventually his uncle told him, and he wrote to Soyer asking – rather diffidently – if he might come over and make his father's acquaintance. Soyer was much moved by the letter, and wrote to ask his son to come over to London to meet him. He clearly remembered Mademoiselle Lamain, but whether he knew she had had his child is not certain. It would seem out of character for the warm-hearted Soyer to abandon his love and their offspring if he knew, though, as the *Memoirs* point out ". . . he had formed an attachment which was rather troublesome to him. He was then only twenty years of age, thoughtless, of light and rather timid disposition."

He was certainly no longer timid or thoughtless – though his disposition was still, in many respects 'light'. The son came to London, he and Soyer liked each other and they kept in close touch after he returned to France.

A couple of years later Soyer decided to go to Paris as he wanted to acknowledge his son according to French law, so that he could inherit after his father's death, and thus the young M. Lamain became Alexis Soyer the second.

The young Alexis remained in France, but history doesn't relate what he did there, or where he lived. However he had a son, Nicolas, who followed in grandfather's footsteps in many ways. Nicolas Soyer was also meant to go into the church, but, like his grandfather, decided such a life was not for him, and he apprenticed himself to a chef in Clermont Ferrand. Eventually he, too, came to London and his most successful job was also to be chef at a London club, this time Brooks's, where he worked at the beginning of this century.

Like his grandfather he was an enthusiast and an innovator. In his case it was to publicise and perfect the art of paperbag cookery, and in 1911 he published a book called, simply, *Paper Bag Cookery* which was an instant success. He went to great trouble to get everything *right* – the main problem he encountered was to find the best sort of paper for the bags, and eventually the firm of Spicer and Co. produced one that was satisfactory, and Soyer paper bags were sold quite widely. The writing shows the same quirks that his grandfather had, and phrases such as "I would get up at two in the morning in order that I might put my paper bag to some fresh test," sound very much like Alexis.

I have not been able to find out much about Nicolas, and there is no mention of his having had any children, so it seems that the Soyer line died with him, as when Alexis visited his old home town of Meaux he was sad to find that all his family there was dead.

It is interesting to speculate on the origins of the family. The surname Soyer seems unfamiliar to French people, and the only other person I have ever heard of with the name was a Russian Jewish painter, Raphael Soyer, who emigrated to the United States, and who died quite recently. The first names of Alexis and Nicolas certainly sound as much Russian as French, and it is possible that the family may have originally been Russian Jews who, some time in the 18th century, emigrated to France. It is true that Alexis' family must have been Catholics as he was meant for the church, but they might well have become completely assimilated by his time. Certainly his own colourful personality, with his creativity, love of personal ornament, appreciation of the arts, could seem to have more in common with a Disraeli than a shopkeeper in a northern provincial town in France.

What views Alexis Soyer held on religious or philosophical matters doesn't emerge, though probably not very strong ones, as although brought up as a Catholic in France he was married in a Protestant church in London and was installed as a Mason, and became a 'Grand Scotch Knight, Knight of the Sword and the East, Grand Prince of Jerusalem, Knight of the East and West, and a Sovereign Prince Rose Croix of Heredom, etc., etc."

These high degrees in the Order seemed not to be generally known, as, according to Messrs Volant and Warren (his ancient and late secretary respectively) there should have been more pomp and ceremony at his funeral if his fellow Masons had been there.

Decoration for the Gastronomic Regenerator

V

Cooks and Books

There have been famous cooks and famous writers on cooking through the ages, but during the 19th century great changes took place both of style and content.

Until this time the great chefs – Vatel and Carême being two of the best known – were cooks in private households. The restaurant as we know it today did not exist. There were taverns and coaching inns which provided food of a kind and lodging when required, but these were used more out of necessity than pleasure, and it was not until after the Revolution in France that the modern type of restaurant began to emerge.

In the first instance the word *restaurant* denoted a kind of restoring soup, much favoured by Parisians, and it was not until the late 18th century that a tavern was opened in that city, using the name *Restaurant* where the soup and other modest dishes – so long as they did not rival the *râgouts* made by the *traiteurs*, or cooked meat shops – could be obtained.

The French adopted and adapted the English idea of the tavern in the new *restaurants* and gradually a new kind of eating house was established in France; the name *restaurant* stuck, and was eventually accepted everywhere.

It was from this time, too, that we get the name *Bistro*, as after the wars with Napoleon the troops occupying Paris included Russians, who, when they wanted to eat something in a hurry would call out "Bistro! Bistro" – the Russian word for 'quickly', and this then came to mean the small cheap eating place with food ready to eat.

It was a Parisian, Beauvilliers, who, it is said, was the first *restaurateur*, and who started a fashion for the kind of food served in English inns, refined by the French cooks to something grander and more generally acceptable. There were several reasons for this change in eating habits; two of the most important ones being directly attributable to the French Revolution.

After the Revolution there were many civil servants in Paris, who needed somewhere central and congenial to eat at mid-day, and they popularised these new 'English style' taverns in the city, and the other, very pertinent reason was that after the Revolution there were very few grand households where a private *chef* could be employed as had been the custom earlier. This meant that there were skilled *chefs* without employment, so they turned their talents to catering for the public, and starting their own *restaurants*, or, in several cases, coming to England where there were still enough rich employers who were glad to have them. As for the *restaurants*, as we know now, they flourished, and the idea of such an eating house spread all over the world.

Soyer himself easily found employment in a private household when he first came to England, and people such as the Earl of Sefton, the Dukes of Cambridge and York, Lord Chesterfield, the Marquis of Ailsa all, at some time, employed some well known chef – or one who, because of such employment, *became* famous.

But the increasing importance of the London clubs, with their greater resources and growing membership, attracted chefs away from the private houses, and the food provided by them for club members has, to a very great extent set the pattern for middle class eating habits today.

Soyer doesn't write much about his fellow chefs, or refer to many of them by name, though they must have been a close-knit if competitive group. The two that he does seem to have been friendly with were Charles Pierce, who he met when he was working with Mr Lloyd at Oswestry at the beginning of his career, and Louis Eustache Ude, a fellow countryman, who also spent most of his working life in England.

Ude probably came to England as a result of the French Revolution, though there is not much information about him. But he worked as chef to the Earl of Sefton then to the Duke of York, and eventually became *maître d'hotel* to the new gambling club Crockfords. Soyer makes many references to him and Ude was one of the witnesses at Soyer's wedding in St George's, Hanover Square. He seems to have been a rather bad-tempered man, or at any rate he quarrelled often with his wife, and his own household was filled with dogs, cats and parrots, which when combined with the noise of domestic strife, must have made life for the neighbours very difficult.

Monsieur Ude once gave a disastrous dinner party to celebrate his birthday. As the guests arrived so they were greeted by numerous dogs, some of whom were not particularly friendly disposed, "Thus, one of the guests, in attempting to kick away spiteful 'Azor', stumbled and knocked down one of the dessert plates, cooler and all, from the side-board, and, in trying to save it, went bang over the plate-warmer. His lady trod on 'Tiny's' paw, the scream was awful, the hostess almost fainted; in fact, all was in an uproar for some minutes, until the master, in a stentorian voice, made each dog go into his kennel."

This was only the beginning. One of the guests had been asked to carve the main dish of venison, and put the plate he was about to fill to warm on the spirit-warmer nearby. Alas, the plate cracked, and so did the next one he used the same way, until seven of the plates (which had cost Monsieur Ude two guineas each when he bought them at a sale of the late Duke of York's effects) were ruined. Ude was furious and took much soothing down, and Soyer, always ready with the *bon mot*, drank his health with the toast "that he never break peace with China again". And they then got on with the venison.

But disaster was still with them. One of the guests didn't like his venison and fed some to the unfortunate 'Tiny', who was so greedy for it that he choked himself to death and "the harmony of the evening was thus much disturbed". The other dogs, meanwhile had been busy licking the varnish off the boots of the male guests which afterwards looked as if they had been rubbed with mutton fat.

Ude wrote a book on cookery called *The French Cook*, in which he is scornful of Englishwomen whose palates, he wrote, had been "completely benumbed" by the "Strict diet of the Nursery and boarding school."

Another famous chef contemporary of Soyer was Charles Elme Francatelli, who was of Italian extraction but born in England and educated in France. He, too, was chef to various noble households before joining Crockfords, as had Ude before him. He later became *maître d'hotel* and Chief Cook to the Royal Household, and later still went to the Reform Club, a year or so after Soyer had left.2

It may well have been Francatelli that Soyer was visiting at Windsor on the occasion of the umbrella with the foot-and-a-half hole in it, but he was never mentioned by name. The two men had very similar ideas in many ways, not least in their attitude towards the waste of food – "while he was able to dress the costliest banquets Francatelli was likewise a culinary economist" and he said that he could feed a thousand families a day on the food that was wasted in London. His great culinary weakness was the extravagant use of truffles which he used in any dish he could.

He produced one cookery book at about the same time that Soyer was publishing his. In 1845 came *The Modern Cook*, and later on, in the 1860s, after Soyer was dead, followed *The Cook's Guide and Butler's Assistant*; the *Plain Cookery Book for the Working Classes* (Soyer would have approved of this one particularly), and *The Royal English and Foreign Confectionery Book*.

The Modern Cook is straightforward, practical – and rather dull. The difference between him and Soyer was summed up in a contemporary magazine. "Both as cooks and authors, Soyer and Francatelli have been the last to speak in volumes:

Soyer covering his knife of sacrifice with flowers of poetry, and investing even a *tête de veau a l'Indienne* with a most touching sentiment; while Francatelli performs his task with the grave air of a sacrificing Druid, looking upon dinner as rather a serious consideration, which has more to do with man's progress for evil or good than your mere swallower will allow."

These were professional chefs who wrote cookery books, but at the same time there was a growing number of housewives who wrote books too, often a gathering together of manuscript recipes that had been handed down through family and friends.

A century earlier Hannah Glasse had published her *Art of Cookery Made Plain and Easy* – she is the writer who is supposed to have used the phrase "first catch your hare" which is probably a misinterpretation of skinning or 'casing' a hare –, and Elizabeth Raffald gave us *The Experienced English House-keeper* at the beginning of the 19th century. Both these books were landmarks in cookery writing, but today they seem remote and difficult to understand, partly because of the layout and typeface which still used the long 'S'. Mrs Rundell also published the *New System of Domestic Cookery* at about the same time, and this covered all aspects of household management as well as cooking, and was really the first book of this kind. In it she urges housewives to encourage their cooks to save the scraps from their elaborate dinners to give the starving poor of the cities, and gives good advice on the making and saving of soup for such poor.

However, the great advance in cookery writing came with the publication of Eliza Acton's *Modern Cookery for Private Families* in 1845, the year before Soyer published his *Gastronomic Regenerator*, and to my mind Eliza Acton was the most significant of all Soyer's contemporaries.

Eliza Acton was the daughter of a brewer and born in Sussex, but the family moved back to Suffolk from where they originated. She went to France for her health and obviously became interested in 'foreign' food, which is reflected in her writings. She was going to marry a French officer but that didn't come off and she returned home to live with a married sister – who had a baby soon afterwards, and there are indications that this child may in fact have been Eliza's, discreetly absorbed into the family. Apart from that possible lapse she seemed the model of English middle class spinsterhood, living quietly in London and writing ladylike poetry which was published, but which was not very good. She went to her publisher with more poems, and was told to go away and write something more useful – like a cookery book. So she did. She spent a good deal of her life in Tonbridge in Kent, where her family seemed to have some connection with the school there, and various of her recipes indicate this in their names. Her cookery book was reprinted many times and was the standard work until about the end of the century when Mrs Beeton – who used a great many ideas from both Acton and Soyer and was less interesting than either – took the stage.

Acton was significant for many reasons. First of all she wrote clearly and her recipes are easy to follow today. She was not cooking for a vast household so the amounts given in the recipes are suitable for the smaller families of today with none of the extravagance of "take six dozen eggs". But more significantly she was the first cookery writer to itemise clearly the ingredients used, and the time taken to prepare and cook the dish. Up until then writers had given the method of cooking, but the ingredients were left rather vague. "Take some butter, put sufficient flour . . . " and so on, but not with Miss Acton. Everything was precisely detailed, and in case there was any doubt in the reader's mind they were summed up at the end of each recipe. It is more usual in today's cookery writing to list the ingredients at the beginning, but Eliza Acton's method is just as good and her ideas and methods are perfectly usable now. Many of the dishes were of her own devising, and some were taken from friends, in which case she often put that although she hadn't tried the dish herself, she was in no doubt that it would be good. A delightful sense of humour comes through the writings and she manages to give her dishes very agreeable names.

Two of her famous recipes are for the "Publisher's Pudding (this pudding can scarcely be made *too rich*)", followed by "The Poor Author's Pudding". There is "The Good Daughter's Mincemeat Pudding", and "The Elegant Economist's Pudding", which is a way of using up left-over Christmas pudding.

These two recipes from her *Modern Cookery* were both excellent, and show her straightforward way of laying out her instructions:

Soles Stewed in Cream

Prepare some very fresh middling-sized soles with exceeding nicety, put them into boiling water slightly salted, and simmer them for two minutes only; lift them out, and let them drain; lay them into a wide stewpan with as much sweet rich cream as will nearly cover them; add a good seasoning of pounded mace, cayenne, and salt; stew the fish softly from six to ten minutes, or until the flesh parts readily from the bones; dish them, stir the juice of half a lemon to the sauce, pour it over the soles, and send them immediately to the table. Some lemon-rind may be boiled in the cream, if approved; and a small teaspoonful of arrow-root, very smoothly mixed with a little milk, may be stirred to the sauce (should it require thickening) before the lemon-juice is added. Turbot and brill also may be dressed by this receipt, time proportioned to their size being of course allowed for them.

Soles, 3 or 4; boiled in water 2 minutes. Cream, half–whole pint; salt, mace, cayenne: fish stewed; 6 to 10 minutes. Juice of half a lemon.

Spring-Stew of Veal

Cut two pounds of veal, free from fat, into small half-inch thick cutlets; flour them well, and fry them in butter with two small cucumbers sliced, sprinkled with pepper, and floured, one moderate sized lettuce, and twenty-four green gooseberries cut open lengthwise and seeded. When the whole is nicely browned, lift it into a thick saucepan, and pour gradually into the pan half a pint, or rather more of boiling water, broth or gravy. Add as much salt and pepper as it requires. Give it a minute's simmer, and pour it over the meat, shaking it well round the pan as this is done. Let the veal stew gently from three quarters of an hour to an hour. A bunch of green onions cut small may be added to the other vegetables if liked; and the veal will eat better, if slightly seasoned with salt and pepper before it is floured; a portion of fat can be left on it if preferred.

Veal 2 lbs; cucumbers 2; lettuce, 1; green gooseberries, 24; water or broth, half a pint or more; three quarters to one hour.

She makes observations as to the richness or otherwise of her dishes, and one gets the feeling that she really did do the work herself, and knew what she was writing about. There are several references in the book to "a Jewish lady of my acquaintance", some of whose recipes she uses, and there is a section on Jewish cookery, which at that time would have been unusual to quote, as Jewish cooking would not, in general, have been incorporated in a standard cookery book, and it was interesting to learn that a year or two ago a facsimile edition of *The Jewish Manual* was published. This had originally appeared at the same time as Acton's *Modern Cookery*, but was published anonymously, "Edited by a Lady", but recent research has discovered that this lady was Lady Montefiore, wife of Sir Moses Montefiore, an important financier and philanthropist, and as some of the Jewish recipes in the Acton book are almost identical to those of Lady Montefiore, it can be assumed that she was the acquaintance referred to by Eliza Acton.

Acton was only concerned with the kitchen and cooking. She did not, like other writers of the time, include sections on household management and etiquette, which is perhaps why her books seem so much more up to date than, say, that of Mrs Beeton, where the household matters now seem so old-fashioned. Eliza Acton was straightforward, easy to understand, and *exact*.

Whether she ever met Soyer has not been revealed. It seems fairly unlikely as their paths went in different directions, though the Montefiores, who were very active in helping the poor and needy, must have known them both – a Montefiore was one of the subscribers to *The Gastronomic*

Regenerator and there is a recipe for a cod dish *à la Montefiore*, presumably created for one of the family – so Acton and Soyer may have met through them. If they did I can't see that they would have *liked* each other much, Soyer was probably too flamboyant a show-off for the more sedate Eliza, but I am sure that they would have respected each other a great deal, for their ideas on food and cooking were very similar in many ways.

Up to the middle of the century cookery and household books were written for the housewife, the servants being mainly illiterate, and the instructions would have been handed on verbally to the cook. But gradually this changed with the greater availability of education, and servants were expected to be able to read and write enough to understand simple instructions. This was why so many books gave such detailed accounts of household matters and often with sanctimonious suggestions for personal hygiene and management of affairs, sometimes even giving ways of doing simple interest for a banking account – it would have been simple interest indeed on the wages of about £8 a year earned at that time. But Soyer and Acton were both writing for the housewife, and one who would do the running of the household herself. It would be the wife who would do some of the work herself or work alongside the cook, they were not meant for the large house with a housekeeper employed to take over the management of the servants and kitchen. There were many young housewives who wanted the easiest and most up to date methods and recipes that would be labour-saving and economical. Not unlike the readers of women's magazines of today. The middle-class housewife starting married life in a very modest way would have been delighted with the ideas and recipes of *Modern Cookery for Private Families*, or *The Modern Housewife*.

In *The Modern Housewife* Soyer gives a good account of middle class eating habits, through the letters of Mrs 'B':

When I was first married and commencing business, and our means were limited, the following was our system of living:

Sunday's dinner –	Roast Beef, Potatoes, Greens and Yorkshire Yorkshire pudding
Monday	Hashed Beef and Potatoes
Tuesday	Broiled Beef and Bones, Vegetables and Spotted Dick Pudding
Wednesday	Fish, if cheap, Chops and Vegetables
Thursday	Boiled Pork, Peas, Pudding and Greens
Friday	Peas Soup, Remains of Pork
Saturday	Stewed Steak with Suet Dumpling

This went on for a couple of years, by which time they had better means, three young men, presumably clerks, to dine with them, and some new ideas gained from a visit to France.

The week's menu was:

Sunday	Pot-au-Feu. Fish – Haunch of Mutton, or a quarter of a Lamb or other good joint – Two Vegetables – Pastry and a Fruit Pudding
Monday	Vermicelli Soup made from the Pot-au-Feu of the day previous. The Bouilli of the Pot-au-Feu – Remains of the Mutton – Two Vegetables – Fruit Tart
Tuesday	Fish – Shoulder of Veal stuffed – Roast Pigeons or Curry – Two Vegetables – Apples with Rice, and light Pastry
Wednesday	Spring Soup – Roast Fowls – Remains of Veal minced, and poached Eggs – Two Vegetables – Rowley Powley Pudding
Thursday	Roast Beef – Remains of Fowl – Two Vegetables – Sweet Omelet
Friday	Fish –Shoulder of Lamb – Miroton of Beef – Two Vegetables – Baked Pudding
Saturday	Mutton Broth – Boiled Neck of Mutton – Liver and Bacon – Two Vegetables – Currant Pudding

Even later, although catering for the same number of people, the style had changed again and Mr and Mrs 'B' dined by themselves unless they had company, as they very often did. By this time their ordinary daily menu was of: "One Soup or Fish, generally alternate – One Remove, either Joint or Poultry – One

Frontispiece for the Modern Housewife, 1848

Entrée – Two Vegetables – Pudding or Tart – a little Dessert." Mrs 'B' goes on to say that although this might seem rather a lot for two people the remains were used for breakfast, lunch, nursery and servants' dinners and that they lived in comfort without waste.

The first book that Soyer wrote was a book of essays called *Délassements Culinaires* published in 1845. This is not really very interesting today, the essays full of rather heavy-handed punning humour, and the only two things worthy of note were the strange portrait of the author as if in a distorting mirror and the scenario for his unperformed ballet *La Fille de l'Orage*. But the following year he produced *The Gastronomic Regenerator*, a large volume of recipes "... which will," he wrote, "enable the most inexperienced cook, *or young lady just commencing housekeeping*, to compose a recherché or economical bill of fare at will." There is more emphasis on the recherché than on the economical in this book, and as it was written when Soyer was at the Reform Club and the subscribers to the book were mainly peers, or at least upper class gentlemen, much of the work is really more for them and their chefs. I would think the young lady starting housekeeping would have been a bit daunted by the famous 'Bouquet de Gibier, or Sporting Nosegay' which is so elegantly illustrated at the beginning of the book. This is a "picturesque mode of keeping game, so as to make them ornamental until they become useful," and more suited perhaps for the country house than the bijou residence in town. And the following recipe is hardly for the novice cook:

Noix de Veau pique au jus (receipt no. 565)

Procure a very white leg of veal from a cow calf, saw off the knuckle, lay the fillet on the table and cut it open without cutting through the meat, that is cut from the bone in the centre under the udder until you cut through the skin, take out the bone, and lay it out, there will be three separate lumps of meat, the largest of which is the noix (or nut); to cut it out press your hand upon it and with a sharp knife cut down close to the skin, separating it from the skin till it comes to the udder, then bring the knife up, lay the piece upon the table the best side downwards and beat it well, trim it of a nice shape, and lard it with pieces of fat bacon two inches long and slender in proportion, cut off the udder and sew it to the side, put a few slices of bacon in a flat stewpan, with two or three onions cut in slices, half a bunch of parsley, two bay-leaves, and a sprig of thyme, lay in the noix, add a pint of white broth, then put the lid on the stewpan, and place it in a moderate oven for three hours, occasionally looking at it, taking care that the gravy does not become dry or burnt, if it becomes dry add a little water to moisten now and then with the gravy; when done, glaze it nicely, slightly colour it with the salamander if required, and lay it on a dish, keep it hot, then pass the gravy through a tammie into a smaller stewpan, set it in the corner of the fire, skim off all the fat, pour it in your dish, and lay the noix in the last moment of serving, or the fat would run, and give the gravy a bad appearance.

The recipe that follows in the book is also for Noix de Veau, served with cauliflower and green peas, and apparently there is no need to "be particular about its being the leg of a cow calf," which must be a relief to the housewife doing the shopping.

On the other hand what could be more simple or delicious than his way of cooking *Saumon à la Pêcheuse*.

Take a slice of thick salmon and make an incision upon each side, cutting it to the bone, put plenty of salt and chopped onion upon it and rub it well in, then oil a sheet of white paper, lay the salmon on it, fold the paper over and crimp it at the edges to keep the steam from escaping, put it on a gridiron over a slow fire, and when done serve it in the paper with pats of butter separate; the person that serves this dish at table should open the paper and place two pats of butter on each slice; it requires to be eaten very hot.

This is the way I cook salmon, using aluminium foil instead of paper, and it is excellent, as it keeps in both moisture and flavour.

There are recipes for elaborate desserts, including one commemorating his ballet and the dancer for whom it was composed – *Cerito's Sultane à la Fille de l'Orage*, and some jokey ones making sponge cakes and preserved fruit to look like joints of meat. There is one for his 'mutton cutlets reform' when the 'meat' is made of sponge, the bones of almonds, with a sauce of pineapple syrup. The centre is filled with lemon ice and the 'mushrooms' are meringues.

Admittedly he does write at the end of this section of the book "End of Receipts for the Table of the Wealthy", before going on to the next bit which is entitled The Kitchen at Home, and, although we have learned that in fact his kitchen at home did not exist, the recipes are much more to the present day taste and style. The style of writing is much more relaxed and chatty, and one can recognise the beginnings of the style of *The Modern Housewife* that followed a year or so later.

He is said to have dictated the recipes for *The Gastonomic Regenerator* to his more literate kitchen maids at the Reform Club, reckoning that if they could understand them then anyone would. That may be so, but I think the maids would have been more at ease in the Kitchen at Home.

The Gastronomic Regenerator was received with tremendous enthusiasm by the public and press. The reviews were favourable, some newspapers giving the book a column of space, and whole magazine articles were devoted to it as the new approach to cooking. "Cold must be the stomach, and compressed must be the lips, that will not glow and smack at the very numeration of the contents," and, "From a portrait, serving as front piece to the volume, we imagine M. Soyer to be an exceedingly intelligent, good-humoured, pleasant fellow." The portrait referred to was one painted by his wife Emma, and there is a rather touching Memoir of her, together with her own self-portrait, at the end of the book.

"It is perhaps the best and most comprehensive system of cookery hitherto offered to the public."

Blackwood's Magazine gave the book a review of some ten pages, in the course of which Soyer is likened to the Duke of Wellington, which I think is taking admiration a bit too far: "*The Gastronomic Regenerator* reminds us of no book so much as the *Despatches* of Arthur Duke of Wellington. The orders of Soyer emanate from a man with a clear, cool, determined mind –

possessing a complete mastery of his weapons and materials.... It may be a matter of dispute whether Wellington or Soyer acquired their knowledge in the face of the hotter fire. They are both great Chiefs – whose mental and intellectual faculties have a wonderful similarity – and whose sayings and doings are characterised by an astonishing resemblance in nerve, perspicuity, vigour and success."

In another paper he is referred to as "The great Napoleon of Gastronomy", so one can choose which comparison one likes. In fact, neither is probably very flattering to a chef, if looked at more closely. Napoleon was said to have watered down his Burgundy, and the Duke of Wellington apparently lived on rice pudding and cold meat, to the extent that his chef, Felix, another of the great cooks of the time, got so cross at producing delicious meals that passed without comment, saying that the Duke wouldn't notice whether chef or kitchen maid had prepared them, that he gave notice and went.

The *Observer* review of *The Gastonomic Regenerator* ended with the paragraph stating that "Monsieur Soyer's volume is full of entertainment and instruction for gastronomic readers. We do not know, however, whether we should not recommend an abridged edition for 'the million', who may not have leisure for all the discursive flights which he takes towards immortality."

Although his next book was not quite the abridged edition suggested, it did go a very long way towards providing for 'the million'. In 1849 he published *The Modern Housewife* which again was an instant success and sold fifteen thousand copies in under nine months. It was very different in style from *The Gastronomic Regenerator*; the recipes are simpler and more straightforward, with continuing emphasis on economy, and the book gives an excellent insight into the domestic life of the middle classes of the time.

It has been suggested that the recipes seemed more like the food that would have been served to his catering staff, using up left-overs from the grander meals upstairs, but I think this is unfair. It went into many editions and was in print for the next fifty years. The *Spectator* wrote "*The Modern Housewife* is the most dramatic of cookery-books; carried on by dialogue, correspondence, and a certain artful arrangement by which two-thirds of an epic – 'action' – is introduced into the didactic work." As with the previous book there were long and flattering reviews in all the papers. But *Fraser's Magazine* devoted eleven pages of the August 1851 edition to a vitriolic attack on it and its author. The review is anonymous, but it reads as if written by someone who knows a lot both about cooking and the author of the book, so it may have been a jealous colleague – it was a review of the twenty-first edition – who had had a book of his own rejected. The author of this attack refers several times to 'quackery', and says that "Mons. Soyer's *Modern Housewife*, otherwise insignificant, becomes very important as an engine of mischief, likely to retard the progress of the science it pretends to expound, on which the greatest of our social blessings – health – so very much depends."

That must have been an unusual view taken as the number of copies sold would indicate. The difference between this book and others of the same period is that a large part of the book is taken up with the correspondence between Hortense (Mrs 'B') and Eloise (Mrs 'L') over domestic matters. Mrs 'B' is a model housewife, herself modelled on a real Mrs Baker, who lived at Bifrons Villa in St John's Wood, and whose skills at household management excited Soyer's very real admiration. The letters between the two ladies give advice from Mrs' B' to her eager but disorganised friend on how to run her house efficiently and economically. I think that if I had been Mrs 'L' (and I have to admit that I am more of a Mrs 'L' than a Mrs 'B') I would have got rather exasperated with her unfailing cheerfulness and efficiency, but there is a lot of useful and amusing stuff in the letters, which range from breakfasts, and how to make toast, through invalid cookery, food for the nursery, and the bachelor's dinner to the Septuagenarian Epicure.

I fancy that Mrs 'L' would have recognised some of her dinner parties in this extract from 'A Table of Errata' written by Thomas Hood at about the same time as *The Modern Housewife*; and that it will strike a sympathetic chord in the heart of many a modern housewife now.

Well! thanks be to Heaven,
The summons is given;
It's only gone seven
  And should have been six;
There's fine overdoing
In roasting and stewing
And victuals past chewing
  To rags and to sticks!

Now then for some blunder,
For nerves to sink under;
I never shall wonder
  Whatever goes ill.
That fish is a riddle!
It's broke in the middle,
A Turbot! a fiddle!
  It's only a Brill!

It's quite over-boiled too,
The butter is oiled too,
The soup is all spoiled too,
  It's nothing but slop.
The smelts looking flabby
The soles are all dabby.
It all is so shabby
  That Cook shall not stop!

Friends flatter and flatter,
I wish they would chatter;
What can be the matter
  That nothing comes next?
How very unpleasant!
Lord! There is the pheasant!
Not wanted at present,
  I'm born to be vext!

> *The veal they all eye it,*
> *But no one will try it,*
> *An Ogre would shy it*
>   *So ruddy as that!*
> *And as for the mutton,*
> *The cold dish it's put on,*
> *Converts to a button*
>   *Each drop of the fat.*
>
> *The beef without mustard!*
> *My fate's to be flustered,*
> *And there comes the custard*
>   *To eat with the hare!*
> *Such flesh, fowl and fishing,*
> *Such waiting and dishing,*
> *I cannot help wishing*
>   *A woman might swear!*
>
> *My troubles come faster!*
> *There's my lord and master*
> *Detects each disaster,*
>   *And hardly can sit:*
> *He cannot help seeing*
> *All things disagreeing;*
> *If he begins d– – ing*
>   *I'm off in a fit.*

The later editions of the book had added details and anecdotes about the ladies and their own fortunes. Mr 'B' made unfortunate financial speculation, and their comfortable position declined, but he did manage to get a position as Head Clerk of the Railway, though this necessitated their moving from the St John's Wood villas to a cottage in Rugby. However, Mrs 'B's' domestic expertise still enabled them to live fairly comfortably, and they had a country girl (who never smiled, but always laughed) to do the hard work. It seems that this reflected the fortune of the real Mrs 'B', who was reported to have "died in hospital" following her husband's difficulties. However, while they were living comfortably in St John's Wood she was able to give detailed descriptions of the typical dinners of the time, and the way that dining changed both in timing and style.

Not long before this time the main meal of the day would have been eaten early in the afternoon as the leisured classes did not rise very early and so lunch was not particularly important. But the middle class Mr B had to go to his office, by omnibus, and got back about five in the evening, so that he wanted to eat after that, and when they had guests it would have been 'late dinner'. Also, there was a marked change in the way that meals were served. Up to the middle of the century it would have been usual to have all the dishes laid out on to the table, sometimes with duplicates at each end, and the guests had to help themselves or their neighbours. This is why the menu plans of the time look so complicated and the meals so vast – diners were not expected to eat *everything* on offer, only what they fancied, or could reach. This was not only cumbersome and extravagant, it also meant that the food was likely to be cold by the time it reached the plates, apart from the problems in having to ask your neighbour to serve your food, as well as taking wine with guests at the other end of the table. A good description of the English dinner party was given by Prince Pückler-Muskau who wrote in his *Tour in England, Ireland and France* that "After the soup is removed, and the covers are taken off, every man helps the dish before him, and offers some of it to his neighbour (the art of carving, which is too much neglected in Germany, forms part of a good English education); if he wishes for anything else, he must ask across the table, or send a servant for it; – a very troublesome custom, in place of which, some of the most elegant travelled gentlemen have adopted the more convenient German fashion of sending the servants round with the dishes.

" It is not usual to take wine without drinking to another person. When you raise your glass, you look fixedly at the one with whom you are drinking, bow your head, and then drink with great gravity. Certainly many of the customs of the South Sea Islanders, which strike us the most, are less ludicrous. It is esteemed a civility to challenge anybody in this way to drink; and a messenger is often sent from one end of the table to the other to announce to B– – that A– – wishes to take wine with him, whereupon each, sometimes with considerable trouble, catches the other's eye, and goes through the ceremony of the prescribed nod with great formality, looking at the moment very like a Chinese Mandarin. If the company is small, and a man has drunk with everybody but happens to wish for more wine, he must wait for the dessert, if he does not find in himself courage enough to brave custom."

Mrs 'B' explains that she likes to use the new method of serving – usually known as *service à la Russe* whereby the dishes were handed round the table to each guest, in the same way as we do today in more formal occasions. This meant that meals became simpler, as it would have been impossible to have so

Table of the wealthy

many dishes as the old style permitted, and although the gentlemen at the ends of the table (not always the host) would still have carved the joint, the whole affair became more manageable.

The style of serving was still under discussion a quarter of a century later, as Jules Gouffe explained in his *Royal Cookery Book*: "There have been endless discussions as to the relative merits of the two systems of serving; named rather arbitrarily, the *à la Française*, the other *à la Russe*. The first consists in setting the whole of a course on the table at once, taking each dish off to serve it; in the second mode, the dishes are brought to the table already cut up, which makes it difficult to present them otherwise than in fragments, set up together again in the best practicable way...

"Both systems have their advantages and disadvantages; the mode of service *à la Française*, the complications and slowness of which have been justly criticised; but in the former system, the necessity of cutting up all the dishes before the guests see them puts an end to the possibilities of decoration, which many cooks turned to so good account, and tends to destroy the tasteful and rich appearance which formerly characterised high-class cookery...

"Nothing is to prevent putting on the table, to dress and deck it as it should be; first, large cold pieces capable of receiving such great richness or ornamentation, also, the removes and hot entrées, which are generally equal to waiting on the dishwarmers without deteriorating.

"In this way the guests, when they sit down, will not be greeted by a table decked out merely with fruit, compôtes, bronze articles of *vertu*, vases of flowers and similar objects, little nourishing in character, and unlikely to act as appetisers, as to ensure justice being done to the dinner about to follow.

"Neither will there be any objection to merely sending round the cut-up dishes which require immediate eating, without seeking to use them for show purposes. By these means the dinner will be sooner and more easily served, and ample time will be obtained to carve the large dishes properly."

That the old method of putting everything on to the table at once could cause difficulties, was shown by an account of the arrest in Scotland of a traveller "with toozy black whiskers" and a parrot nose, both of which gave him an unwholesome appearance.

He was thought to be a spy, as he could speak nothing but French, and had on him a paper that appeared to be a map of the Clyde, with various islands, clearly identifiable. Eventually it was discovered that the poor man was a chef, and the map no more than the setting for a fashionable table for service *à la Française*.

In Mrs 'B's' account of her dinner table she says she employs two servants to wait at table which "gives me an opportunity ot seeing that my guests are properly attended to, and also leisure of taking wine with any gentleman who challenges me".

In spite of the misfortunes, real or fictional, of Mr and Mrs 'B', Soyer produced another book with the same formula of correspondence between the two ladies, though this time the recipes were aimed at the working classes. Thus, with this *Shilling Cookery for the People,* published in 1854, he completed his idea of writing about cookery for the upper-, middle-, and working-classes. If the *Charitable Cookery* is included, for the very poor as well.

The Shilling Cookery went into many editions and, as with his other books, was an instant success. The recipes in it are much more simple and plain than in the other two books but there is a lot of good sense in it, and many of the recipes are more suited to present day tastes for less elaborate food.

There are a lot of good points made about the preparation and cooking of simple dishes – his advice given to an ignorant old crone on how to cook ox-cheek or other tough meat is very sensible, and his way of making such a basic dish as mashed potatoes is excellent: cook them with the skin on, peel them after they are cooked, then take two forks in one hand, with the prongs turned outwards, and break up the potatoes with them, adding butter and milk to taste. This way really does produce good light potatoes, of a better consistency than those done with a potato masher or mechanical device, and is just as quick.

Frontispiece for A Culinary Campaign, 1857

There are two other publications, *A Culinary Campaign* which was not so much a cookery book but more of a memoir of his time in the Crimea, and properly belongs to the account of his time there, and in 1853 came *The Pantropheon*.

After the success of his previous books Soyer had often said that he would like to write a scholarly treatise on the food of the ancient times and *The Pantropheon* was an immense work covering all aspects of eating, drinking and preparation of food. The *Illustrated London News* described "the practical character of the present volume, the method of which is admirable; commencing with agriculture, cereals, grinding of corn, manipulation of flour, frumenta grains, seeds and vegetables. Then follow the kitchen garden, plants used in seasoning, fruits; animal food; the cook and the kitchen; beverages; repasts, and a variety of accessory subjects; all illustrated with *morceaux* of ancient and modern history, and hints of practical value.

"As a book of luxurious reading, abounding in classic anecdote and olden gossip, the 'Pantropheon' will, doubless, become popular."

It is certainly a major work, but lacks the amusing touch of the other books. In 1977 it was republished in facsimile, and Margaret Lane, in her review for the *Daily Telegraph* wrote: "How the endlessly busy and sociable master-chef found time not only to master Latin and Greek but also to delve into the culinary habits of ancient civilisations, to translate their recipes and research their agricultural methods, remains a mystery." There is a list of 3,000 classical references to support his authority, the style is "Exuberantly grandiose" and the favourite adjective, used constantly is "magiric", a new word to me, but according to the O.E.D. it means "pertaining to food". Anyway, the mystery seems to have been resolved. Soyer never wrote the book. He only translated the work of another Frenchman, Adolphe Duhart-Fauvet.

When I was beginning my researches into Soyer's background I was talking to Michael McKirdy of Cook's Books in Rottingdean, knowing that he and his wife are great Soyerphiles – in 1987 they published the facsimile edition of the *Memoirs* of Soyer, upon which I have drawn extensively for anecdote and information – and he produced for me, like a conjuror, a copy of *The Pantropheon* that he had recently bought. On the fly leaf, written in beautiful copperplate is the inscription:

> *Offert*
> *Pauline Duhart-Fauvet*
>   *par l'auteur*
> *son mari bien tendrement Devouée*
> *Adolphe Duhart-Fauvet*

(then in flourishes underneath) *3 Sept 1853 Londres.* and underneath that is written in pencil:

> *Il n'a jamais été dit dans mon contrat de vente du manuscrit français qui le nom seul de M. Soyer illustrarait l'ouvrages.*
>   Ad D-F[1]

Throughout the book are pencil notes in the same hand – sometimes less than perfect, as if the writer were losing his temper.

After the entry for Modern Banquets comes the comment:

> . . . *ces banquets modernes, qui font de mon livre une sorte de manuel de cuisine, on été ajoutés par M. Soyer sans mon autorisation.*
>   Ad D-F[2]

Poor Monsieur Duhart-Fauvet, one can understand the sense of outrage he feels when on the errata page at the end of the index he writes:

[1] These modern banquets, which make my work into a kind of cookery book have been added by M. Soyer without my permission.
[2] It was never said in my contract of sale of the French manuscript that the name of M. Soyer alone would have adorned the work.

Je declare que cet ouvrage, intitulé Pantropheon *a été entièrement composé et ecris par moi en Français. Mon manuscrit, vendu a M. Alexis Soyer, et miserablement traduis en anglais par je ne sais quels manoeuvres litteraires, doit me rapporter, d'après notre contrat: 1, cent trente deux livres dix shillings payés a la livraison de manuscrit: 2, deux cents libres stirling qui me serront guarantie sur les benefices. Londres. 3 Septembre. Adolphe Duhart-Fauvet*[1]

From which it seems quite clear that Soyer had paid to make the translation and should have paid some royalties, but somehow had contrived to get the work accepted as his own.

In the note at the end he refers to his previous books, *The Gastronomic Regenerator* and *The Modern Housewife*, and mentions that he had observed that if anyone were to write a History of Food and Cookery, ". . . it would not only be very interesting, but also an extremely useful production. No one, however, having entertained my suggestion, I determined to undertake the task, and, after several years of deep study and perseverance, have completed this voluminous work." After this is written in the beautiful copperplate an observation to the effect that this is ridiculous to anyone who knows Soyer.

Not much is known about M. Adolphe Duhart-Fauvet except that he was French, but lived in London and he published two books of poetry, *Poèsies Françaises* in 1872, and *Champ de Roses* in 1839. He was obviously not confident of his command of English otherwise he would not have asked Soyer to take on the translation of his book – if his English had been better it might be thought that he was the author of the

---

[1] I declare that this work, entitled *Pantropheon* has been entirely composed and written by me in French. My manuscript, sold to M. Alexis Soyer, and miserably translated into English by I do not know what literary manoeuvres, should have brought to me, after our contract: 1. one hundred and thirty pounds ten shillings paid on delivery of the manuscript; 2. two hundred pounds stirling which were guaranteed to me from the profits. London 3 September. Adolphe Duhart-Fauvet.

savage attack on *The Modern Housewife* in *Fraser's Magazine* of 1855, as he certainly had no reason to feel kindly towards Soyer.

At first it seems out of character for Soyer to play such a dirty trick on anyone. He was a practical joker it is true, but not a malicious one. However, this book came along at a time when he was in a very poor financial state, following the collapse of his ill-fated Symposium at the Great Exhibition, of which more later, and he was never one to take kindly to following other people's suggestions. In the *Memoirs* there is reference to "one characteristic peculiarity in his character which made him reject many advantageous offers, for the simple reason that the idea did not spring from his own brain". He had to be the leading light in anything he did. The *Memoirs* tell us that he was indeed contemplating a book on the history of food at the time he published *The Modern Housewife*, and presumably when the offer of translating *The Pantropheon* came along it was more than he could resist, not to add to it and embellish it so that he could make it appear his own. Certainly there is some of his own work in it, a conversation with Lord M– H– (Lord Marcus Hill) and Soyer, and the observations he makes on *garum*, a brine used by the Romans to pickle fish, for instance, and most of the illustrations are by M. Volant, his secretary and joint author of the *Memoirs*.. Significantly the *Memoirs* are far more reticent about *The Pantropheon* than about the other books Soyer wrote, and it seems clear that he was not in fact the author, though he passed the book off as his own, which was less than generous of him.

Soyer had made plans for a College of Domestic Economy, adapted to the instruction and the wants of the upper-, middle-, and lower-classes, for, as he wrote in the proposals for such an establishment, "Many females enter into the great business of their lives – the management of a household – in perfect ignorance of its duties; which has precisely the same results as if a man entered into a trade or profession of which he was totally ignorant and unable to direct his servants." He made elaborate plans so that the students would be in classes of five, to "be selected so that the students of each will be the children of those whose family or guardians are acquainted with each other, or occupy the same station in society."

It may be that this attempt both at segregation of the social classes, on one hand, and integration, by making provision for all kinds of females from every walk of life on the other, proved too much for Victorian society to accept. Whatever the reason, nothing came of it. A pity, as not only would many of his good ideas have been introduced to a wider audience, but the students would probably have had a good deal of enjoyment out of it too.

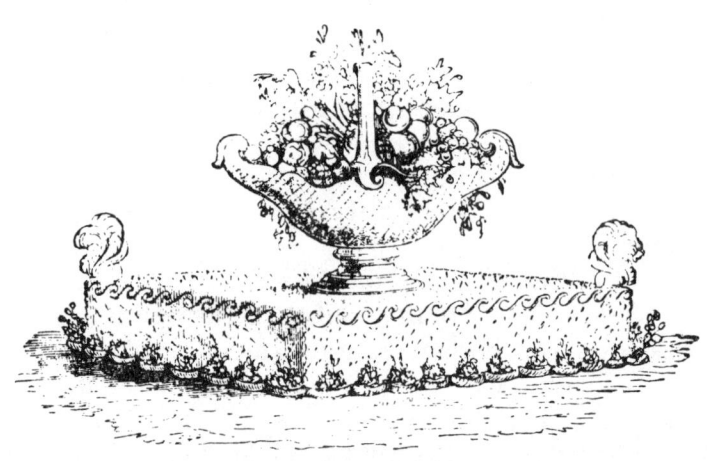

The St James's Cake

VI
Stoves and Sauces

The mid-19th century must have been an exciting time to live in – there were so many ideas and so much confidence around. Inventions came tumbling out of the minds of people of all kinds, not only the factory inventions of the Industrial Revolution, but domestic ones to make life easier, cosmetic ones to make every woman more beautiful, and so on. A look at any of the magazines or newspapers of the time will show the dotty ingenuity of some of these ideas. And of course, Soyer, with his endlessly fertile brain was always coming out with something new.

One of his first inventions was the Tendon Separator, "its object to relieve carvers, more or less proficient, and must become indispensable for the use of all cooks and poulterers in disjointing the volatile species previous to trussing, roasting, or boiling." At that time it fell to the lot of the guests at the ends of the table to carve for the company, and as Soyer pointed out it was all right for the clever carver, "but to a person inexperienced, the notion of being placed at either end of the table, to stay the ravenous appetite of some of the guests, causes such a nervous excitement, that it is not an uncommon thing to see the splashing of sauce and gravy on those around – perchance the sudden appearance of an unfortunate limb flying with terrific velocity on a lady's dress, the whole of the company being thus thrown into confusion – the poor carver's apologies received with black looks, and the harmony of the party placed in jeopardy." The Tendon Separator was similar to the present-day kitchen shears, and could cut through tendon and joint with ease, and must indeed have been useful as described.

He produced a patent Egg-Boiling Machine, a Vegetable Drainer, which was a saucepan fitted with a perforated pan and drainer so that not only, he said, did it save time and did away with "the tedious method of fishing the greens or cabbage out of the saucepan," but it also meant that the valuable vegetable water was not thrown away (which might also clog up the drains, to the annoyance of the household). His Chimney Screw Jack was a sort of metal bracket, cheap to buy, that would fit on to the mantel-shelf and be adjusted at will so that the joint on the suspended spit could be set nearer or further away from the fire. For although there was much more use made of the closed oven at this time, the jack, or spit was still in use for roasting, often with a Dutch oven. The method that today we call 'roasting' would have been described by Soyer as 'baking'.

He did produce an 'Improved Baking Dish', and a 'Baking-Stewing-Pan', which cooked meat in a way he described as semi-roasting, and this useful pan was "so constructed that it may be hung over the fire, or placed on the hob, or steamed or boiled in a stewpan (as you would a pudding boiled in a basin), or in a cottage or baker's oven." The idea was to keep the lid on the pan to keep in the goodness of the food, and he constructed a lock and key for this lid so that no one would lift it during the cooking period, much the same today with a pressure cooker at one end of the cooking scale, or a slow cooker at the other. There was a Magic Coffee Pot – and later on when he was in the Crimea, the Scutari Tea Pot, which was a large kind of kettle in which was a cylindrical filter to hold the tea which was then infused when the boiling water was added. The same principle as the small teaspoon infusers still on sale now. His Cooking Clock is exactly the same as those in use today – "By the aid of this little alarm the housewife will be able to time her joints, pies, and puddings, to an instant. By

Soyer's Modern Housewife's Kitchen Apparatus

winding it up and setting the hand back, starting from twelve, to the time required for the article to cook." – familiar to present day cooks.

All these objects seem every-day to us now, but at the time they were something new and exciting, as was the free-standing stove. In *The Modern Housewife* there is a long chapter on household affairs when Mrs 'B' describes all the new appliances available in her kitchen, such as washing machine, drying machine and ironing stove. But what she is really proud of is Soyer's Modern Housewife's Kitchen Apparatus. The gas, she said, was a great economy, as the fire is lit only when it was needed; not, as with charcoal or coal having to be kept going all the time. The new stove is described in detail: "It combines a roasting fire; circulating hot water boiler, oven, and hot plate, all heated by one fire; the boiler heats the water at the top of the house for the baths, and which can be laid on into any room. The advantage is that it gives more room in the kitchen, of being able to walk all round it, there is also different degrees of heat on the hot plate, and room for the *bain-marie* pan; the smoke goes under the floor into the old chimney. . . . it would. . . . be most valuable in hotels and taverns; in a cottage the linen could be dried around it without danger from fire." She also allows a note of superiority to creep in; "not having gas near your cottage you cannot adopt it," she writes to Mrs 'L'. He also produced a massive gas range, capable of producing dinner for 80 people which he named the Phidomageireion.

But the domestic appliances that made his name, and by which he is still known now, were the field kitchen stove used in the Army from the time of the Crimea up to the second world war, about which more later, and Soyer's Magic Stove. "The most useful, ingenious, simple, and economical *Cooking Apparatus* ever invented, by which, for a trifle, any person may cook their own breakfast, dinner or supper, without the aid of fuel. It may be used in the parlour of the wealthy, the office of the merchant, the studio of the artist, or the attic of the humble. By all it will be found a most useful article of furniture; and must become a household favourite." This ingenious device can be seen at the fascinating Domestic Appliances Gallery at the Science Museum in South Kensington with an explanation as to how it works. The idea is that the reservoir above a lamp contains the spirits of wine which, when lit, vapourise and by some process that I do not understand, pass through a burner into the stove which is connected to it. It is the forerunner of the methylated spirit stove that waiters use to heat or flambé dishes at restaurant tables (now, I think, fired by bottled gas, but the same principle applies).

He was obviously delighted by the success of this stove, and I am sure he thought it entirely his own invention, for, as noted before, he was unwilling to accept other people's ideas unless he could make them his own. But, as with *The Pantropheon*, the idea for the Magic Stove was *not* his own, but belonged to a Chevalier Lemolt, who visited Soyer and "brought with him a small stove, not above six inches in diameter, heated by spirits of wine, ingeniously contrived. M. Soyer at once perceived the importance of this little apparatus, and, very shortly afterwards, it was brought out, with valuable improvements, as Soyer's Magic Stove."

I suppose he reckoned that the 'valuable improvements' he made justified his claiming it as his own invention, but seems to emphasise his extreme vanity, and wish for public acclaim. And it was the acclaim he was after, not money, to which he often seemed indifferent, and apparently he made nothing from the Stove. It was manufactured by Messrs Gardner of Charing Cross, who a few months after the launch of the stove, registered their own modified design stating that they were the owners of the Magic Stove. Soyer apparently got no royalties, nor, I think, did the poor Chevalier Lemolt, of whom nothing more is heard.

The public loved it, and it was described as being so clean in use that "a gentleman may cook his steak or chop on his study table; or a lady may have it among her crochet or other work."

As often happened his admirers were moved to celebrate his achievements in verse:

> *Soyer, no more to one small class confined,*
> *With Magic Stove now cooks for all mankind;*
> *Pall Mall but just sufficed for his rehearsal,*
> *The world his club, his guests are universal.*

And of course, there are numerous stories about the use and advantages of the new invention. One was that a traveller to France had the Magic Stove with him, but was told at the customs that as it was hardware it could not be taken into the country. Nothing daunted, the Englishman said it was his kitchen, fixed up the stove, produced (from where, one wonders?) two egg and breadcrumbed cutlets *and* a frying pan, and cooked them under the astonished gaze of the *douaniers*, who of course, were so impressed that the traveller was allowed to continue on his way accompanied by stove, and pan.

Soyer also tried out the Magic Stove on some friends at a

Cooking on the Magic Stove in the Acropolis, Athens

picnic. Having promised to provide the food he turned up at the appointed spot with a mass of raw meat, much to the anxiety of the guests. But – as if they couldn't have guessed – the Magic Stove came into action, and to their astonished delight, they were able to have a hot dinner "in the fields, far away from the humblest cottage hearth."

Ballooning was a popular craze at the time, and one balloonist, Lieutenant Gale, was so sure of his skills that he asked Soyer to let him demonstrate the use of the Magic Stove in his balloon. But even Soyer, for once showing sense over his desire for publicity, thought it would be unsafe, saying that he didn't think there would be many customers for stoves in the clouds, and refused. The Lieutenant seems to have been a very unfortunate fellow – he had spent some years as a coastguard on the north coast of Ireland, and "had passed a good many years of his life in the United States, following what avocation I know not, but failing, apparently, to realise any substantial profits therefrom. . . . he was a dreamer of dreams . . . was miserably poor; he had a huge family of young children, and was wholly incompetent to advance his views, or make interest, in influential quarters." He was thus described by George Augustus Sala, himself interested in ballooning, and who helped the poor Lieutenant in his idea of making a lecture tour – also unsuccessful. Lieutenant Gale was full of ideas for taking a ship to the Arctic, thence to use a balloon to "survey the vast tracts of icy deserts", hoping to find some trace of the lost Arctic Expedition of Sir John Franklin and his fellow explorers. Not surprisingly he got no backing for this idea and shortly afterwards the poor fellow fell out of his balloon when over Bordeaux, and his body was found half-devoured by dogs. Which seems the sort of unhappy fate appropriate to such a poor-doer.

Another venue for demonstrating the value of the Magic Stove was much more to Soyer's taste. The Marquis of Normanby, a public figure and politician, who was a member of the Reform Club, where he had met Soyer, who he admired greatly, went off to Egypt with some friends, and was able to climb to the top of the Pyramid Cheops with the stove and appropriate raw materials, in order to cook dinner for his companions. Apparently successfully, as the event was recorded by drawings done on the spot. I'm sure that Soyer would have wished to be there himself, though he was able to

Distinguished gourmets dining out on (top of) Cheops

SOYER'S SAUCE.

demonstrate the versatility of his invention by providing a meal at the top of the Acropolis while on a visit to Athens.

There was also the Pagodatique entrée dish; a large bowl surrounded by four smaller bowls, intended to be used for a main dish to be placed in the central bowl with different sauces as accompaniment in the surrounding ones. The elaborate construction was never a commercial success, although Soyer used it himself in his banquets. It was cumbersome, and as it was supposed to be made of silver, expensive as well.

It has often been said that we are a nation of sixty religions and only one sauce, but in Soyer's time this was far from true. I am not sure about the number of religions, but sauces there were in plenty. English type sauces that is; the kind that we add to our food after it is cooked, and when it is on our plates. The French would perhaps regard these – if they considered them at all – as garnishes or relishes, not sauces in the true sense, which are an essential part of the dish, and when the meat or fish or whatever the main ingredient, is cooked or served in the sauce. The French sauce would be based on meat juices if it were to be a brown sauce, or on cream and eggs for a white sauce. The English sauces are based on vinegar and ketchup, and designed more to add sharpness to the food than to enhance an existing flavour.

Most of our sauces are legacies from Empire and East India Company days, for Indian Army or civil servants brought back ideas and flavours from the Far East, based on the spicy food to which they had become accustomed. The word ketchup, or catsup, as it often used to be spelled, comes from the Chinese word *ke-tsiap*, which was the brine used to pickle fish. Originally ketchup here was not a tomato sauce, as tomatoes were looked upon with a good deal of suspicion until well into the 19th century, as no one knew if they were fruit or vegetable, but would have been made with mushrooms, and mushroom ketchup was the base for many of the proprietory brands of sauces that found their way to the markets in Soyer's time.

The famous Worcestershire sauce started at the beginning of the last century, when Sir Marcus Sandys returned home from his term as Governor of Bengal, and asked his local chemists Mr Lea and Mr Perrins to make up the formula for him. They did so well out of this that the two chemists bought the recipe for themselves and set up a sauce factory instead of a pharmacy. Most of these sauces were given the name of their inventor, Harvey's sauce and Quinn's sauce being two of the most popular, and Goodall's made Yorkshire Relish, and Burgess made their still famous Anchovy Sauce. Each brand had its own fancy bottle and distinctive label, some even being distinguished enough to have a little silver label, like a miniature wine label to hang round the neck of the cut-glass bottles in the fashionable Victorian cruets. Most of the original sauces were thin, pungent liquids, and had a base of such things as shallots, vinegar, mushroom or walnut ketchup and anchovies. Gradually different types came in, such as H.P., with a mixture of fruits added to the rest – more like chutney – which also had its origins in the East, from the Hindu word *Chatni*, a side dish of fruits and spices to be used as a garnish for curries.

As one can guess, Soyer wasn't going to confine himself to inventing mechanical devices for the kitchen, but had to busy himself with sauces as well.

There was Soyer's Sauce Succulente, "Thick, pulpy and of a reddish brown colour. It contains *vinegar*, a considerable quantity of *tomato, wheat-flour, shallots, garlic, red-currant jelly*, several herbs etc. In flavour it is exceedingly delicate and agreeable." Or so the advertisement claimed. Then there was Soyer's Relish, the Aromatic Mustard and the Sultana's Sauce. All sold in jolly little bottles, with a portrait of the chef on the label.

How all these sauces differed from each other is a mystery, and it may be that it was too much for Soyer himself and he produced Soyer's Sauces, "One expressly for the Ladies, and the other for the Gentlemen", sold at 2s 6d for half a pint. The Relish was the best known, and my guess is that it was a development of all the other sauces which he then ceased to bother about.

Punch greeted the new sauces with glee as "A NEW DEVOURING ELEMENT – you all know Soyer the Philanthropist, who pretends to be so full of his fellow-creatures? Can you doubt it after the following? Read it, and feel 'like goose's flesh' all over! 'Soyer's New Sauce for Ladies and Gentlemen!!!' Was there ever such a cannibal? And this is the man who would wish to redress our society and our dinner! Why, it is regularly setting man against wife, son against mother-in-law, pauper against beadle, boots against cook! No lady, no gentleman is safe. The aristocracy is on the verge of the sauce-boat. We denounce Soyer as the greatest *traiteur* in England, or even Ireland, and the latter, is say, at present, an immense deal." This last reference, of course, being to his soup-kitchens.

Mr Crosse and Mr Blackwell were his good friends, and their firm made and marketed all his sauces – and later on when he went to the Crimea, it was to these two friends that he entrusted Emma's pictures for safe-keeping. Unfortunately, although the firm still exists, in name at least, there have been so many changes in ownership and organisation that all records of their dealings with Soyer have been lost or destroyed. Perhaps some of the pictures went too, as there seems no trace of them any more.

The sauces were on sale for many years, though now seem to have disappeared completely. They must have been similar to the H.P. or O.K. type of sauces still very much in demand. George Augustus Sala, who became a close friend at the time of the Great Exhibition, wrote that Soyer received quite a lot of money from Crosse and Blackwell for the sauces, and that he regretted having had, but having lost, the prescription, which he remembered had had a foundation of garlic.

At about the same time as the Relish, Soyer came across a fruit drink called 'Tortoni's Anana', "but as the flavour was very indifferent, the sale was limited: therefore, as M. Soyer's name was considered of great importance to a new drink, he agreed to become a partner, and the celebrated 'Nectar' was then introduced by him." I don't know if this was another instance of Soyer taking over someone else's idea and promoting it as his own, but this time there does seem to have been some kind of deal struck with the originator, a company formed, and an acquaintance of the Stock Exchange put up £1,000 towards the nectar manufacture. There seems to have been some disagreement between the people involved; the new partner took over the running of the enterprise, and Signor Tortoni, if that was his name, appeared to be pushed out. Soyer sold his share for £850, but the nectar continued popular.

It was a mixture of the juices of fruits such as raspberry, quince, apple and lemon, made effervescent, so that it beat all the "lemonade, orangeade, citronade, soda-water, sherry-cobbler, sherbet, Carrara-water, Seltzer, or Vichy water we ever tasted." It also inspired the following verse:

When I arise in feverish pain,
And feel a giddiness of brain
What brings back my health again?
                Soyer's Nectar.

Walking in the cool parterre,
Fête champêtre, or fancy fair,
What regales the debonair?
                Soyer's Nectar.

If with nausea at the sight
Of dainties, which all else delight,
What restores my appetite?
                Soyer's Nectar.

When at ball, or masquerade,
Whirling round the gay parade,
What revives when spirits fade?
                Soyer's Nectar.

It sounds like a more palatable cross between Alka-Seltzer and Underburg. Perhaps someone ought to market it again.

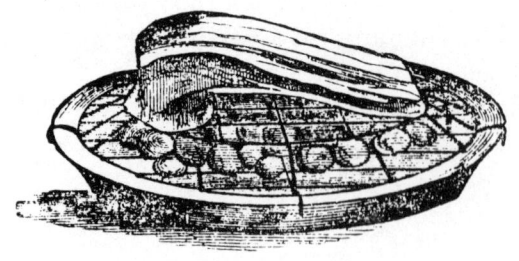

Soyer's improved baking dish

VII
The Exhibitionist

In the middle of the nineteenth century one event, in particular, unified the whole country. The Great Exhibition of 1851 symbolised the age of progress that had so changed the life and appearance of the nation. The building that held the exhibition was magnificent in itself – it was *Punch* that christened it the Crystal Palace – and the thousands of people of all nationalities and all walks of life who visited it must have been both impressive and impressed.

The guiding spirit behind the idea of such an extensive display was Albert, the Prince Consort. He was a hard-working man, a patron and lover of the arts, and he tried to learn fully about any subject that interested him, or which he had to know about in the course of his duty. He was largely responsible for forming a Royal Commission, which, together with the Society of Arts, was to organise funds and set up the machinery for the vast enterprise. There had, of course, been exhibitions before, both in this country and in Europe, but nothing on the scale planned for this Great Exhibition at the Crystal Palace.

Albert was a prime mover in the planning, but much of the actual organisation and the setting up of the scheme was due to Henry Cole. Cole was a civil servant – at one time he worked with Rowland Hill and helped to introduce the Penny Post – and a talented water-colourist and typographer, and if Albert provided the ideas it was Cole who helped to put them into action.

The names of the Commissioners were made public in January 1850, with the Prince as their President. Hyde Park was chosen as the site for the exhibition, and sixteen acres set aside for the building and its surroundings, and 1st May 1851 was chosen as the opening date. Throughout 1850 plans and designs were submitted to the Commissioners, and eventually those of Joseph Paxton were chosen. Paxton was already well known for the great conservatory he had designed for the Duke of Devonshire at Chatsworth, and his proposed exhibition hall was a greatly enlarged version of this glasshouse. A lot of work had to be done in the time and by January 1851 over two thousand men were employed in building the vast glass palace, which when finished was to measure nearly two thousand feet in length, and over four hundred in width. Many trees in the park had to be cut down to make way for it, but three large elms were left to grow inside, under the highest part of the arched transept, which measured a hundred feet to the topmost pane of glass, and there were other, smaller groups of trees allowed to grow in other parts of the building. Although the structure was of iron and wood, the main feature was the amount of glass used, and it must have looked a magnificent sight when it was all lit up. It must also have been extremely hot inside.

Only a few years later, in 1855, came the great Paris Exhibition, remembered especially for the classification of clarets, which has influenced wine buying ever since. In his book on the Second Empire, Philip Guedalla describes how "The sightseers stood staring at the marvels of science in the Palais de l'Industrie; but it was all a shade more modish, a thought less improving than the gleaming monument of good intentions with which Prince Albert had obliterated Hyde Park four years before." A gleaming monument of good intentions is probably a good description of the Crystal Palace, but very likely the Paris Exhibition of 1855 would not have been so modish if the Parisians had not felt that they had to outdo and improve upon the earlier one in Hyde Park.

The Commissioners also bought Gore House, opposite the

Hyde Park site, with an additional seventy acres of land surrounding it, and this is where Alexis Soyer comes in.

Gore House stood where the Albert Hall now is, and was an elegant stucco house, set back from the road behind a large wall and approached through impressive gates. The garden was full of flowering shrubs, roses and fruit trees, and it was quiet and secluded. The house had once been the home of William Wilberforce, the reformer and philanthropist, but more recently it had been lived in by the Countess of Blessington, who had made it a famous *salon* and meeting place for every one who was anyone. Poets, painters, politicians, writers and people of fashion all met there; Disraeli, Dickens, Wellington, Thackeray were all frequent visitors, and the whole place must have sparkled with wit, wisdom and gossip.

Lady Blessington spent much of her married life in a strange *ménage à trois* with her husband and the elegant Count d'Orsay, and later, in widowhood, with the Count and his wife, who was her stepdaughter. The Count d'Orsay seems to have had an equivocal position in the household as both Earl and Countess were much attached to him, and the Earl, in his will, more or less bequeathed his daughter, Lady Harriet, to d'Orsay as his bride. Not surprisingly the marriage was not a success, and the lady left her husband, but d'Orsay and Lady Blessington continued their strange alliance, with a relationship, it seems, not as lovers, but more of mother and son. D'Orsay was very popular, extremely elegant and fashionable – he created, or at least made modish, the *paletot*, a sort of loose outer garment, which Soyer also favoured. He was an athlete, a gambler, an artist, witty, extravagant and selfish.

Lady Blessington was a great beauty, a famous hostess, and a successful author. In the end she was ruined financially by d'Orsay. Their lavish entertainments in Gore House, d'Orsay's gambling debts and tailors' bills must have been wildly expensive; in the end d'Orsay didn't dare go out of doors during the day for fear of his creditors, and in the spring of 1849 the house and contents had to be sold to cover all the debts. D'Orsay fled to France; Lady Blessington stayed behind to settle the financial commitments, then went to Paris herself, where she died only a few months later.

A GREAT DEAL has been written about the Great Exhibition and its wonders, but here we are mainly concerned with the role that Soyer had to play at this time.

After he left the Reform Club Soyer didn't have regular employment but was often sought after for public banquets and dinners for which he received much publicity and praise. The two most notable banquets were at Exeter, given by the Royal Agricultural Society for a thousand guests, and the other, significant for his future career, at York. Early in 1850 the Prince Consort and the Lord Mayor of London had given a banquet at the Mansion House for provincial mayors from all over Britain, in order to interest them in the forthcoming exhibition, and to enlist their support. The mayors responded by giving the Prince and the Lord Mayor a banquet in return, held at the Guildhall in York, which received a great deal of publicity, and Soyer was responsible for the catering. After this it was natural that he should think about the possibility of applying for the catering contract at the Great Exhibition, and was approached to see if he would be interested. However there were so many restrictions laid down as to what could or could not be provided, that it wouldn't have suited him at all as he realised, so in the end he didn't tender for it.

Indeed the terms for the catering contract as reported in *The Times* makes the whole enterprise seem quite unwelcoming, and not at all in the style that Soyer would have wished, or been able, to accept. There was to be no Sunday opening, no dogs or smoking allowed, no intoxicating liquor of any kind – though it was compulsory for glasses of filtered water to be available at no charge – and no cooking or heating apparatus, except for boiling water for tea or coffee. And there were to be no seats.

Three different areas in the building were allocated for refreshments, and visitors were expected to go to whichever they chose, and select and eat their refreshments standing up, or, I suppose sitting on the ground, as they were not allowed to take their food outside those specified areas. One of these areas was to provide ices, sandwiches, pastries and so on, with tea, coffee or soft drinks, and the other two offered rather plainer food, such as bread and cheese, with cocoa, ginger beer or spruce beer to drink. The Commissioners stressed that they didn't want to create a tavern atmosphere at the Exhibition, as apparently there had been an embarrassing incident shortly before, when the Horticultural Society had had wine available at one of its shows. It appears that our catering provisions and public eating habits have not changed greatly over the last century and a half.

In the end Messrs Schweppes paid £5,000 for the catering contract and subcontracted with two other firms. It was a profitable exercise and, according to the accounts, almost a million Bath buns were sold, and almost as many plain ones, thirty-odd tons of ham, a hundred tons of meat and thirty thousand quarts of cream. The ices were immensely popular – in the heat of the building they must have been the only cool things there.

Not surprisingly there were numerous complaints about the quantity and quality of the food, the overcharging and the lack of cleanliness. *The Times* published a long series of letters from dissatisfied customers, the correspondence started by 'A Distressed Agriculturist', who complained that he and his party had been charged one shilling for the sixpenny ices, and threepence instead of twopence for a slice of cake. He asked to see the price list and it was found that he had been overcharged, but "It must have been a mistake on the waiter's part"; but he went on to say that it had happened the day before and the day after, after which the price list went missing. Others suggested that a price list, written in different languages, should be framed and displayed where it could be seen easily, to "remove from the ladies in waiting the

The refreshment room at the Great Exhibition

temptation of exacting more than is right", and others complained of the personal appearance of the waiting staff, and the contractor would "do well in case of increasing business to have relays of washed damsels, if he wishes to see his eatables well digested." *Punch* wrote about "the wonderful efforts of art, which have been met within the Refreshment Room . . . our attention was . . . particularly directed to a section of ham sandwich, containing a small deposit of ham, so beautifully attenuated as to be worthy of weighing by the machine capable of appreciating the weight of a millionth part of a scruple. We have also met, occasionally, with an object – not very rare in the metropolis but still, in its way, curious – namely, a lukewarm ice."

Some people overcame the problems by taking "good wholesome sandwiches, made at home, and a small vial of *eau de vie*, with which I flavour the excellent water . . . the only good thing to be got there." The heat, the noise and the crowded conditions with nowhere to sit must have been trying, and bearing all this in mind it seemed a good idea to provide an alternative place for refreshment, and Soyer, with financial help from friends, took a lease on Gore House and its grounds, which, being situated immediately opposite the Exhibition itself were easy to reach, but outside the Exhibition's jurisdiction, so there was no problem about what could or could not be provided.

Soyer had no Committee to restrain him as he had had at the Reform Club, so was able to let his imagination really run wild on this new toy of his, and, as often happened, went over the top in fantasy and extravagance, naming his enterprise THE GASTRONOMIC SYMPOSIUM OF ALL NATIONS, and he enlisted the help of his friend George Augustus Sala (who had also been a frequent visitor to Lady Blessington's *salon*) to design it.

Soyer produced a prospectus for the Symposium, on "Satin paper, the edges delicately printed green and scalloped", promising great things to the ticket holders (tickets one guinea, or a family ticket, admitting five, was three guineas), and claiming that he would be able to provide dinners and refreshments for five or six thousand people, and "the charges for which will not preclude persons of every station from partaking of the hospitality of the Maison Soyer."

Sala joined in the spirit of the idea, and went to town on the decorations, even though, as he admitted afterwards, he disliked some of the schemes and despised himself for doing them.

He had already published a series of caricatures and sketches entitled *The Great Exhibition Wot is to Be*; drawings of public figures of the day, depicted with large heads and very small bodies. Soyer had been included in these sketches and this so pleased him that nothing would do but that Sala should do the same sort of decoration on the great staircase of Gore House with a panorama of such characters. Sala wrote later that "Soyer, who was nothing if not fantastic, and to a certain extent quackish, insisted, to my reluctance and no small disgust, in calling it "The Grand Macedoine of All Nations; being a

Demisemitragicomipanodicosmopolytolyofanofunnisym-
posiorama, or
Suchagettingupstairstothegreatexhibition of 1851."

There were fantastic animals; griffins, dragons, mastodens, elephants, camels and so on, and public figures such as the Duke of Wellington, Victor Hugo, Disraeli, Napoleon, General Tom Thumb, George Cruikshank and countless others. Thackeray, writing in *Punch*, described it as "A staircase ascending, emblazoned with the magic heiroglyphics, and strange allegoric images. In everything that the Briton does lurks a deep meaning – the vice of his nobility, the quarrels of his priests, the peculiarities of his tutors, are here dramatised; a Pope, a Cardinal appear among fantastic devils – the romancers of the day figure with their attributes – the statesmen of the three kingdoms with their various systems – friends, dragons, monsters curl and writhe through the multitudinous heiroglyphic, and typify the fate that perhaps menaces, the venomous enemies that empoison the country." Disraeli, visiting the Symposium, dressed with enough gorgeous waistcoat and gold chains to excite Soyer's envy and admiration, presented Soyer with a quotation from one of his novels, printed on white watered silk with a gold fringe. Sala says he forgets what the quotation was, "but it contained an allusion to the Beautiful." Disraeli was fascinated by the Symposium and, in one of his many letters to Lady Londonderry wrote: "The most wonderful thing in the world is Soyer's Symposium, which he has made out of Gore House and its gardens – poor Lady Blessington's former abode. It is impossible to conceive anything more various and fantastical – dinner saloons of every kind of size and character – Turkish, ancient Greek, Louis-Quinze, roofs of Italian trellices with bunches of waxen grapes hanging over your head and longing to be plucked. One room presents a cavern near the north pole – its roof covered with icicles which drip upon the

Gore House, Soyer's Symposium

guests, but then it's only rose-water or eau-de-cologne – in the distance a beautiful scene where, I think, they must discover Sir John Franklin. In the gardens, amid a thousand other things as wild and gay, is a grotto, where a live Ondine is to preside, of matchless beauty, guarding a fountain with a 100 jets each of which when touched by her fills your glass with maraschino, curaçao or some kind of liqueur."

Sala also produced an immense and detailed catalogue of the Symposium, for the whole of Gore House and its garden were completely transformed. There were tents and alcoves all over the garden and "a stalactitic pagoda with double windows in which gold and silver fish floated"; there was an exhibition of Madame Soyer's paintings along with some by the Count d'Orsay, perhaps left behind when the house had been sold. More ground was bought, to be named the Pré d'Orsay, which had in it "grassy pyramids supporting vases of flowers and Watteau-like statues." There was the Vestibule of the *Fille de l'Orage*, named after Soyer's undance-able ballet; the Washington Refreshment Room, for the dispensing of every sort of American beverage; Emerald Pyramids of Morning Dew, and countless other attractions such as the Hall of Architectural Wonders, in which were depicted the Tower of Pisa, the Eddystone Lighthouse, the Mosque of St Sophia and goodness knows what else. A huge tent had been put up in the garden which he named the Baronial Hall, – Thackeray said, "I should rather have thought that it was a marquee," when it was shown off to him.

Gore House had originally been a place of elegance, and though in its new guise it must have been great fun, *Punch* summed it up by writing:

> *Soyer, the praise thy skill deserves*
>   *Is perfectly immense,*
> *For nice discernment in the nerves*
>   *Of gustatory sense.*
>
> *But now Gore House hath been by thee*
>   *So glaringly defaced,*
> *However good thy palate be,*
>   *We must dispute thy taste.*

In fact, *Punch* gave the Symposium a great deal of publicity, largely through Thackeray, who wrote as M. Gobemouche, an unsophisticated Frenchman who marvelled at everything. In one account M. Gobemouche takes a cab "through the romantic village of Kinsington, and through the Bridge of Chevaliers", intending to go to the Exhibition Hall. When the cab set him down he paid his shilling to go in and found "The chambers of this marvellous place are decorated in various styles, each dedicated to a nation. One room flames in crimson and yellow, surmounted by a vast golden sun, which you see, in regarding it, must be the chamber of the East. Another, decorated with stalactites and piled with looking-glass and eternal snow, at once suggests Kamschatka or the North Pole. In a third apartment, the Chinese dragons and lanterns display their fantastic blazons; while in a fourth, under a canopy of midnight stars, surrounded by waving palm-trees, we feel ourselves at once to be in a primeval forest of Brazil, or else in a scene of fairy – I know not which; – the eye is dazzled, the brain is feverous, in beholding so much of wonders." Later on M. Gobemouche comes across "a gentleman in a flowing robe and a singular cap, whom I had mistaken for a Chinese or an enchanter . . . I muse, I pause, I meditate. Where have I seen that face? Where noted that mien, that cap? Ah, I have it! – in the books devoted to gastronomic regeneration, on the flasks of sauce called Relish. This is not the Crystal Palace that I see – this is the rival wonder – yes, this is the Symposium of all Nations, and yonder is ALEXIS SOYER!"

Indeed it did become the rival to the Exhibition, and thousands of people flocked in to enjoy themselves. The enjoyment being the greater I imagine, because, after a good deal of consideration, the Magistrates had not only allowed a licence for wine and spirits, but also for music and dancing – which later became one of the reasons for Soyer's downfall. There were also places to sit down, in the house or in the shady garden.

The visitors averaged about a thousand a day, and of course, there were mixed reports and comments on the wonders offered both to the eye and to the palate. Not everybody was satisfied and it would have been an impossible task to cater properly for both the less well-off family parties, and the aristocratic diners who were entertained in some of the private rooms. Although he would have made more profit from the posh dinners, Soyer was, as always, conscious that not everyone had a lot of money to spend, and at the suggestion of a friend he had a translation of one of Martial's epigrams painted over the doorway which read: "Say how many you are, and at what cost you wish to dine; you need say nothing more, your dinner is settled," and it was possible to say, "I wish to dine with four friends at seven shillings each," and suitable fare was provided.

Soyer hoped that he would be able to continue to run the

restaurant after the Crystal Palace closed, and he was always on the look-out for new attractions, and called on the support of Jullien, a popular musician of the time to try to build a winter garden in the grounds, though this never came to anything. But, "Various bands of musical performers, singers, black or Ethopian serenaders (of the most comic power), theatricals, balloons, games of different kinds, succeeded each other with rapidity."

The balloons were not the decorative party kind, but balloons for the more daring to ascend in. This was still a popular pastime, even though the intrepid Lieutenant Gale had perished in his, and Sala was intrigued enough to go along to see this latest craze of Soyer, which was to introduce a new kind of balloon; "... cylindrical rather than spheroidal in form; that is to say it resembled a huge horizontally-sailing sausage instead of a vertically-directed pear with the stalk undermost." Sala watched the balloon being prepared for flight, but although a distinguished public figure had promised to come along for a ride in the horizontal sausage and the crowds gathered to watch the ascent, he didn't appear. No one else was willing to take his place, but Soyer eventually persuaded the reluctant Sala to go up instead, in company with Mr Chambers, "an aged aeronaut", his son and one other person. The idea was to float over Brompton and Fulham Road and to scatter leaflets advertising the Symposium. Unfortunately Mr Chambers was so busy undoing all the decorations hanging round the outside of the balloon that he forgot to loosen the handkerchief that was used to close the neck of the balloon until it was airborne, as when it reached a certain height the hot gas had to be allowed to escape. When the intrepid travellers had reached the height of a mile, and were over Fulham church, the balloon burst, and they fell like a stone for half a mile. Fortunately Mr Chambers managed to control the balloon by somehow cutting at the ropes so that part of the fabric flew up to form a kind of parachute which slowed the descent. Eventually they landed, much to the consternation of the workers there, among the cabbages in a market garden, shaken but not hurt.

One of the wonders of the Symposium, reported in *The Times* was a "covered gallery 130 yards long, in which is a table, reaching from one end to the other, and a tablecloth of commensurate dimensions. The place swarms with attendant pages and etc., and preparations seem to have been made to furnish refreshments to all the nations of the earth." But a month or two afterwards there was another report to the effect that, "On Sunday evening some evil-disposed person penetrated to the Encampment of All Nations, in the Symposium, and succeeded in cutting off and carrying away 25 yards of the monster tablecloth which formed one of the attractions of Gore House, and was certainly a triumph of British manufacture." It must also have been a triumph of British skills that someone should both cut and take away such a large amount of tablecloth without being detected in that busy gathering.

An advertisement appeared in the newspapers for Soyer's Modern Arabian Nights: ". . . being the thousand and second night of those Oriental Entertainments in the Jewelled Garden of Aladdin – Mons. Soyer begs to inform the nobility, gentry and public, that having just obtained Aladdin's Wonderful Lamp, he will, through its magic influence, present a continuation of those Fairy Tales on the 18th inst. To produce the extraordinary effect of enchantment the doors will not open in the evening until 9 o'clock. Carriages to enter at the first gate near the Crystal Palace. Single tickets 7s 6d, double ticket 10s 6d." He also advertised that the entrance fee to the Symposium would be returned in refreshments – which goes some way to explaining why the Symposium proved such an expensive place to keep going.

No wonder it was popular; there was something for everybody. The nobility and gentry came for dinners and the spectacle, and the public for the cheaper refreshments and the fun.

In the July there was a reception for a deputation of French workmen over to see the Exhibition. During the dinner there were many "toasts and sentiments... expressive of aspirations towards peace and unity among nations, but owing to the want of practice in these prandial demonstrations on the part of M. Soyer's guests, there was more enthusiasm exhibited than order or intelligibility... however the best feeling prevailed throughout, and the gentlemen of the deputation appeared delighted at the manner in which they had been entertained, and their sentiments of peace and fraternity echoed." It sounds as if that was exactly the kind of occasion that the Royal Commissioners were seeking to avoid when they forbade alcohol in the Crystal Palace.

There was also a banquet given for the foreign press, about which *Punch* wrote that there was "no doubt that the feast was worthy of the event. Indeed the *Morning Chronicle* assures its patient subscribers that after the roast beef was placed upon the table 'description became hopeless! Imagination might do something; but experience alone could convey an idea adequate to the occasion!' M. Soyer made a speech, very fully reported by the *Chronicle*, nevertheless, the cook's best thing was omitted. It was this: 'Why', asked M. Soyer. 'Why is this dinner the reverse of an *omelette soufflée*?' Everybody gave it up. 'Because,' said the cook, 'an *omelette soufflée* is puffed to be eaten: now the dinner is eaten to be puffed'." The Crystal Palace closed in the autumn of 1851, but if Soyer had managed his affairs better it might well have been possible for him to continue his establishment at Gore House as he wanted. Unfortunately, in the September he had made arrangements for a party of two hundred people from the country, respectably headed by the local parson, to come over to the Symposium for dinner after they had had enough of the Great Exhibition. "As soon as the dinner was over, these country people spread about the ground, and enjoyed themselves over the entire premises – some drinking at the various bars, others skipping about to the bands of music; in fact taking as much pleasure as they could for the few hours they had to remain." It all sounds harmless good fun, but there were several hundred other visitors in the grounds as well, who were animated and noisy and the whole place was *en fête*. Unfortunately it was at this time that Soyer and his colleague Jullien had decided to ask for a renewal of the licence in order to keep the place going through the winter, and the magistrate chose this particular evening to make his inspection to see if it was the right sort of place. Apparently he was deeply shocked to see people enjoying themselves so much, and decided that an orgy, such as this appeared to be, made Gore House into "a receptacle of the commonest description". It became clear that the licence would not be renewed, particularly as a music and dancing licence had been applied for. If it had been a straightforward restaurant licence things might have been different. As it was, Soyer withdrew his application and wrote anguished letters to the press seeking to clear his name of having managed a disorderly house, and he abruptly closed the whole establishment.

Many people, particularly the tradesmen, thought that the sudden closure must mean that he had got himself into deep financial trouble and started to take proceedings against him. However, a notice soon appeared to the effect that those with claims should apply to Soyer's office, and within a few months he had settled everything and paid everyone.

The Symposium had been open for almost six months, and about a thousand people a day "had partaken of the good cheer provided", but, although £21,000 had been taken, the expenses came to much more than that, and at the end Soyer found himself with a deficit of £7,000 and he could never understand why, as he had worked so hard. But considering how feckless he was with money, and how much he must have spent in setting the whole affair up in the first place, it is not really surprising. If he had had good advisers, or a manager who would have looked after the finance properly, Gore House might well have continued as famous and fashionable as it had been in Lady Blessington's time. But Soyer was more easily able to infect his friends with his enthusiasms than they were able to instil a little responsibility into him. Though after this failure, he was sensible enough to refuse to start a restaurant in the City, although he had been urged to do so.

It was about this time that he was working on *The Pantropheon*, and possibly it was because he had got himself into such low water financially that he passed the work off as his own, as he must have made quite a lot of money from the sales of the book.

The whole Symposium episode shows the strengths and weaknesses of Soyer's character: he was hugely inventive and imaginative; he had great organising ability and was generous to a degree and liked to give good value for money; he disregarded financial matters – the advertisement offering the entrance fee back in refreshments was an indication of this; he was vain and adored publicity, and unless he had a very strict budget to work to, as he had with his soup kitchens or at the Reform, he indulged his whims without thought. And I would have loved to visit his Symposium.

Soyer's pagoda entrée dish

VIII
Culinary Campaign

The sudden closure of the Grand Symposium of All Nations was a blow to Soyer – to his pocket and to his prestige. He was left with a great many debts, and no particular occupation. He paid off the debts and made quite a bit of money from the publication of *The Pantropheon*, though, as it now appears, this was money that he really had little right to claim. But this still left him with time on his hands; something that was not at all to his liking.

However, the poor were ever present, and he returned to his earlier schemes of providing soup kitchens, and opened one in Farringdon Road, and another in Leicester Square. There was a ball to raise money to support these ventures, with music provided by Jullien, his associate in the ill-fated Symposium. This also helped to provide a Christmas dinner for twenty-two thousand of the very poor at Ham Yard, when a whole ox was roasted by gas, which was still quite an innovation. There were nine thousand pounds of meat, over three hundred pies of various kinds, one weighing over sixty pounds, and five thousand pounds of plum pudding, as well as packages of tea, coffee, sugar and nuts to be given away.

Of course he was in demand for providing dinners for his various patrons, and made plans for a restaurant at the Exhibition that was to be presented in Paris in 1855.

Also, at this time in the early 1850s the scandalous details about the state of canned meat provided for the Navy were made public, and Soyer was asked to investigate, and look into the whole matter of preserving food for long voyages. He accepted this assignment with enthusiasm, and found much wrong with the whole method of preserving and canning meat, not least the actual contents of the canisters, and out of six thousand cans over five thousand were condemned – these were taken out to sea and sunk off Spithead; where it was later reported that a lot of the fish died. He found that there was too much water and offal in the cans which made the meat putrid, and suggested that a better way of providing the necessary liquid was to have one can containing broth alone, provided for every dozen can of solid meat. Much of the advice he gave was common sense and the Navy had the sense to accept it.

The next year or so went on in much the same way, and life for Soyer was fairly uneventful. But a great deal was happening in the life of the country, for England was muddling herself into a war that could and should have been avoided.

Much has been written, and will continue to be written, about the Crimean War – and this does not attempt in any way to be another account of it. Historians agree on the main point that this war, characterised by private heroism and public ineptitude, need never have happened. As A.N. Wilson wrote in his life of Tolstoy, who was fighting in the Russian Army in the Crimea, the war was "completely pointless and manifestly avoidable".

The five powers, Britain, France, Russia, Prussia and Austria, quarrelled over the 'sick man of Europe' – the Turkish Ottoman Empire. Russia wanted a warm water port, and Britain needed to be strong in the Eastern Mediterranean, as the Suez Canal had already been planned, and she did not want Russia too dominant in that area. Turkey had a great deal of influence in the Balkans, and there was also the question of the Holy Places, particularly in Jerusalem, which were protected jointly by France and Russia. France had recently taken up the claims of the Latin monks there to gain greater control over these Holy Places, and the Turks appeared willing to accept this, which was not in Russia's interests. If Russia controlled Turkey she could then control the Black Sea and the Eastern Mediterranean.

Threats, counter-threats, misunderstandings and muddled diplomacy, all combined to get Britain and France, together with the Turks, into war against Russia, which started in March 1854: a war that was to last two damaging years.

The British Government, having arrived at the point of war, seemed completely unable to cope with the realities of conducting it. There had been no major war since Waterloo, and the Army had been reduced over the years, and was ill-equipped. None of the senior officers had been involved in much actual fighting, and many of them were elderly. Lord Raglan had been only twenty-seven at Waterloo, but was sixty-six by the time he was appointed Commander-in-Chief of the Crimea. Lords Lucan and Cardigan were both in their fifties (and although they were related by marriage, they did not speak to each other, which made command even more difficult).

But the Crimean War was significant, not only for the advanced years of the commanders, but because, for the first time in history, the public at home was aware of the events on the war area, almost as they happened. *The Times*, under its then editor, Delane, was able to send correspondents to the actual battle zones, and thanks to the inventions of cables and telegraphs, the news of the conditions and conduct of the war was available in London very quickly, and it was in great measure due to the most famous of the correspondents, William Howard Russell, that Florence Nightingale and, later on, Alexis Soyer, went on their respective missions, with results that went far beyond the war itself.

The Crimean Peninsula has a summer climate that is benign and delightful, and the area has long been appreciated as a holiday resort. Perhaps this was why the Government sent out its Army so ill-equipped, either thinking the war would be over before winter set in, or, more likely, not realising that the winters were as hard and bleak as the summers were inviting. Indeed one letter to *The Times* suggested that the soldiers were moaning about nothing as surely the climate in winter was no worse than that of Dijon.

The Army was originally sent out to Bulgaria, with few supplies or proper transport. Disease, particularly dysentery and cholera, took a terrible toll, and the difficulties of keeping the men fed, warm, and sheltered seemed impossible. Supplies were sent out, but because of bureaucratic incompetence were either shunted off into a warehouse and never seen again, or even sent back. *The Times* reported that during the first winter a consignment of thick fur coats had been despatched, but because no official letter came with them the Quartermaster General's Department refused to take them. And so it went on. By the autumn the Army was in the Crimea itself, and the conditions were getting steadily worse.

There was no room there for a base hospital, so the sick and wounded had to be transported across the Black Sea to Scutari on the Turkish mainland – some three hundred miles away, and an uncomfortable voyage of several days.

All this was relayed to a horrified public by Russell and his colleagues, and conditions were brought home even more vividly by the heart-breaking photographs so painstakingly taken by the remarkable Roger Fenton.

The conditions at the General Hospital and the hastily built Barracks Hospital at Scutari were appalling, and in the autumn of 1854 Florence Nightingale and a motley collection of women, ranging from nuns to drunks, went out, at the Government's request, to try to bring some order to the chaos.

The story of Florence Nightingale and her efforts are well known. She managed to get order and routine established in the hospitals, but not without a good deal of opposition, and only in the matter of basic nursing but not so much of diet, – though one private soldier writing home at Christmas said in a letter published in the *Guardian*, that he lived like a king on a diet that included "two pints of tea, one pint port wine, one pint of arrowroot and one pint of porter" as well as the choice between a fowl or one pound of mutton chops. He also said that as he had not been paid a halfpenny since he had been in the army he didn't know if he could find the postage for the letter. I think he can't have been that badly wounded, or perhaps the daily intake of a pint of port wine and one of porter kept him in a gently euphoric state.

More typical was a letter, not from the hospital, but signed simply "A Crimean" that appeared in *The Times* in January 1855, which acknowledged with appreciation all the good wishes "which many benevolent and patriotic persons are sending out to us poor devils who have the prospect of wintering out here", but goes on to say that "There is one public character who has it in his power to do us a really good turn, and that is by publishing in *The Times* a receipt or two of how to concoct into a palatable shape the eternal ration of pork and biscuit which is issued to us, and with which we are heartily tired. For my part, if the issue of pork goes on much longer I am afraid I shall soon begin to grunt – the bristles have certainly come out very strong. M. Soyer is the man I allude to as the public character; and I am sure he will give us the benefit of his professional advice."

M. Soyer could not, of course, ignore such a plea, and within the next few days had replied to *The Times* with half a dozen of his recipes, confident that they would "be found practical, economical and nutritious, so far as the simple ingredients used will admit of having regulated, as near as possible, each recipe according to the daily distribution of food, which I see by letters generally consists of half a pound of salt pork and beef, two ounces of rice and six ounces of biscuit."

All these appear in the section for recipes for 'A Squad, outpost, or Picket of Men' published in his *Culinary Campaign*, the following being a fair example:

Stewed Fresh Beef and Rice

Put an ounce of fat in a pot, cut half a pound of meat in large dice, add a teaspoonful of salt, half one of sugar, an onion sliced; put on the fire to stew for fifteen minutes, stirring occasionally, then add two ounces of rice, a pint of water, stew gently till done, and serve. Any savoury herb will improve the flavour. Fresh pork, veal or mutton, may be done the same way, and half a pound of potatoes used instead of the rice, and as rations are served out for three days, the whole of the provisions may be cooked at once, as it will keep for some days this time of the year, and is easily warmed up again.

It may have been this letter that roused his interest in the dietary deficiencies of the Army, for following Russell's despatch in *The Times* of the 29th January 1855 in which he wrote, "∴ it is only since Dr Menzies' departure that Miss Nightingale has succeeded in getting a portion of her nurses regularly installed at the General Hospital, where hitherto they have been tolerated but not encouraged," and a day or so

Soyer's Crimea teapot

later he wrote, "When I wrote my last letter I was under the impression that Miss Nightingale had received permission to establish an extra diet kitchen at the General Hospital, but I find that I was mistaken, for when she made the application in Dr Menzies' time it was refused. She is now about to renew her request, and I hope, not withstanding Dr Lawson's appointment, with better success."

These despatches led to a letter from Soyer in which he wrote that "although the kitchen under the superintendence of Miss Nightingale affords so much relief, the system of management at the large one in the Barrack Hospital is far from being perfect. I purpose offering my services gratuitously, and proceeding direct to Scutari for a short time, at my own personal expense, to regulate that important department, if the Government will honour me with their confidence, and grant the full power of acting according to my own knowledge and experience in such matters."

This decision seemed to have been made on the spur of the moment, after a play at the Drury Lane Theatre, when he was sitting waiting for some friends to join him at dinner. He had made no approach to the Government nor consulted with anyone as to the advisability or possibility of such a venture.

Although he wrote and sent his letter late at night, it was in *The Times* by the morning, and within a day or two he had a summons to visit the Duchess of Sutherland at her home in Stafford House, as she was interested in his idea, and wished to help him to get the necessary Governmental backing. When Soyer visited her he found various influential people there, not least the Duke of Argyll who promised to take his ideas to the Ministerial Council forthwith. Soyer gives an account in his *Culinary Campaign*; "Well," said the Duke, addressing the Duchess of Sutherland, "you must excuse me leaving now, as I have but a short time to get to Downing Street" – piece of dialogue which, like much in the *Culinary Campaign* reads as if it had been written by Daisy Ashford. However, it produced the desired effect, and Lord Panmure, the Secretary for War, agreed to see Soyer at the War Office the following day.

There was a discussion as to the best method that could be found to improve the diet and amenities of the troops, and one point that Soyer raised was that the small tin camp kettle that was in general use in the Army was too small and extravagant of fuel to be of much use, and he promised to try to think up a better cooking appliance. He wrote, "Having heard that no regular kitchens had been established there, I was anxious to have a simple apparatus to take out with me of which I understood the working, and which might be put in action immediately on my arrival. In a very short time I hit upon an idea which I thought could be easily carried out, and would answer perfectly."

I doubt if the inspiration came quite as suddenly as that, but he must have recalled the soup kitchens he had established in Dublin several years before, when he had said that the boilers he had had made then could be adapted to use for large numbers – even an army.

Anyway, he took his ideas to the manufacturers who promised – and delivered – a scale model in two days. He took this back to Lord Panmure, gained his approval, collected various letters of introduction, and announced he would be ready to start by the next mail. While he was at the War Office a gentleman came up to him and asked if he had taken out a patent on the stove, to which Soyer replied that he had not, but that he would have his name on them. The gentleman urged him to patent them as the design would be worth a great deal of money, but Soyer, always more concerned with fame than fortune, said that he would not wish it to be thought that he was expecting payment for his services, so that the stove design was given *pro bono publico*.

He needed a secretary to accompany him on his journey, and among others, approached George AugustusSala, who declined – and afterwards regretted it. Others were asked, but Russell had done his job too well, and the thought of the terrible conditions and disease rampant in the Crimea was too daunting. He could find no one willing to go with him until he bumped into a coloured friend, known only as T.G., who

Soyer's Field Stove

considered the matter for two hours then pronounced himself ready to set forth the same evening, and they went down to Folkestone for the night to await the steamer for Boulogne.

It was at Folkestone that Soyer lost his pocket-book which had in it most of his cash and all his letters of introduction. Panic, of course followed, and T.G. was sent back to London to see if the pocket-book had been left there. But soon after he had gone Soyer found the pocket-book had wedged itself into a corner of the bed, so he sent a telegraph saying "Stop a gentleman of colour – it's all right." By the time the train had reached Tonbridge all the station staff there were shouting "Stop the gentleman of colour", successfully enough for T.G. to hop out of the London bound train just in time to catch the train back to Folkestone and the steamer.

They stayed the next night in Boulogne and there received the news that Nicholas I, the Tsar of Russia had died, but unfortunately the war machine had been too firmly set in action for hostilities to cease and for negotiations with his successor.

Their journey continued to Marseilles (where Soyer was delighted with the *bouillabaisse* which he said belonged as completely to Marseilles as the whitebait to Greenwich). They called at Ajaccio, apparently with the sole object of visiting the kitchens of Napoleon I, and eventually on to Athens, where Soyer lost no time in climbing to the top of the Acropolis with his Magic Stove to cook a *petit déjeûner à la fourchette*, then – at last – they reached the Bosporus and Scutari, with its two hospitals.

As soon as possible Soyer let everyone know of his arrival, not least Lady Stratford de Redcliffe, the wife of the British Ambassador there, and Lord William Paulet, the Brigadier General, already known to Soyer from his time in Ireland, and who was to be very helpful to Soyer during his Crimean stay. The time Soyer had spent at the Reform Club was very useful to him, as it had brought him in contact with many of the people, soldiers and civilians, that he was to meet, which must have eased his path considerably. Among his acquaintances was Mr Charles Bracebridge, who was a close friend of Florence Nightingale, and with his wife Selina had gone with her to Scutari where their help was welcomed.

The two hospitals in Scutari – the General Hospital, which had been in use before the war, and the Barrack Hospital, hastily erected out of necessity as the casualties came pouring in – were both overcrowded and ill-equipped, though the kitchen facilities were marginally better at the old General Hospital.

Miss Nightingale gave Soyer a conducted tour of the hospitals, and from their first meeting there was a feeling of mutual respect and understanding. They were both professionals at their respective jobs, and knew that they would be able to work together.

Florence Nightingale had installed 'diet kitchens' to provide special food for the most severely sick, but she had had such difficulties in getting herself and her nurses accepted by the doctors and senior officers, that she had had to concentrate on the actual nursing conditions first, and as the kitchens were looked after by soldiers, who had no knowledge of cooking, and the stoves were fired by bad quality charcoal, they were always full of smoke and fumes and the food usually burnt.

There were, however, two kitchens that had previously been used by the Turks which Soyer found to be possible, though the boilers were in sad need of repair and relining. They were also used in turn for the tea, coffee and soup, so unless the cleaning was very rigorous it seems certain that one liquid would have tasted much like another.

But Soyer's first major task was to identify the routine, if any such existed, about the feeding arrangements, and the rations allowance. As all the patients were on different allowances, according to their state of health, this was confusing, to say the least. Also the quality of all the foodstuff, except for the good bread, was very poor and the cooking methods worse. The meat was tied very tightly to a piece of wood and dunked into the boilers and cooked fast, so that the outside was in rags, and the inside still half raw. Also, as it was served without any seasoning it was completely tasteless. On his first visit Soyer noticed that the men all ate their meat before their soup, and asked the reason, to be told simply, "We have only one plate." He suggested that the meat should be cut into small pieces and served with the soup allowance poured over it, which would be more palatable and also help to keep the meat hot.

The next days he busied himself with making the rations into well-seasoned soup, even though he had to use the untinned boilers in which to make it, and he instructed the orderlies in a better method of cooking their meat. Each orderly had an allowance of meat to cook, and in order to remember which portion belonged to whom, after the meat had been tied to the piece of wood it was marked: "Upon inspection I found that they had a most curious way of marking their different lots. Some used a piece of red cloth cut from an old jacket; others half a dozen old buttons tied together; old knives, forks, scissors, etc., but one in particular had hit upon an idea which could not fail to meet with our entire approval. The discovery of this brilliant idea was greeted with shouts of laughter from Miss Nightingale, the doctors, and myself. It consisted in tying a pair of old snuffers to the lot.

The barrack hospital kitchen, Scutari

All this rubbish was daily boiled with the meat, but probably required more cooking. On telling the man with the snuffers that it was a very dirty trick to put such things in the soup, the reply was – "How can it be dirty, Sir? Sure they have been boiling this last month."

When the meal was over, Soyer found the copper boilers to be full of the meat broth, with about three inches of fat on the top. He asked what happened to it, to be told that it was all thrown away as it was only the water in which the beef had been cooked, and was good for nothing. He was really shocked by this, and scooped off ladles of fat to be allowed to cool, as he said it was far better than the rank and expensive local butter, and the next day he showed the orderlies how to use it and the good-for-nothing liquid to make the basis of soup.

Tea was made in more or less the same way as the meat was cooked; an allowance of tea was put into a cloth and thrown into hot water, but the bundle was tied up so tightly that the tea couldn't infuse properly at all, – and this led to Soyer's Scutari teapot, which he described as "more of a happy thought than an invention", which was a large kettle with a filter in the centre to hold the tea (and which could also be used for coffee), which made good clear tea and yielded about a quarter more than the old method.

During this time Soyer had had to commute from Constantinople across the Bosporus each day, as the house allocated to him had not been finished. He found this rather tedious, and the water he considered a 'whimsical stream' that could be very rough. However, after he had been there for a few weeks or so, his Kiosque, as he called it, was ready, and he moved into Soyer House, Cambridge Street, near the Scutari Grand Champ des Morts. An impressive address even if the building was modest.

His reorganisation of the various kitchens, in the General Hospital, the Barracks Hospital and the convalescent home at Kululee some distance away, went according to plan. His ideas were mainly common sense planning, the instruction of the orderlies in the preparation and cooking of the food, and constant pressure on the authorities to provide basic amenities. It had been the pattern for orderlies to cook for a week or so, then return to other duties, which meant that there was little continuity in the kitchen, and no one was able to learn proper skills. Soyer had his own group of cooks who had accompanied him, and with their help, and the fact that he was able to appoint one of the sergeants as a regular overseer, meant that a more acceptable pattern, both of culinary skill and cleanliness, soon emerged. He planned a grand opening of the Scutari kitchens to which he wanted to invite the heads of the medical departments, as well as any eminent people whom he could persuade to come along.

He had not been at all well since he arrived in the area, and seemed to be suffering from a mild form of dysentery, but he got worse a day or so before the appointed Grand Opening. He described it himself as a kind of brain fever without any of its symptoms: "Although I was quite conscious of what I had to do, I was entirely incapable of doing it, or of ordering anything or directing any one." The doctors prescribed rest, and indeed, seeing how untiringly he had worked, under such dreadful conditions, it is not surprising that he felt ill, from sheer exhaustion. However, he recovered in time to put his plan into effect, which was to make samples of the diets made under his instruction, alongside the old kind prepared by the unskilled orderlies. These were in numbered basins so that a comparison could be made. The doctors were asked to try the dishes first, then all the other guests, headed by Lord William Paulet and about a hundred others, though some who wished to attend were prevented by the bad weather from crossing the Bosporus from Constantinople. Nevertheless, there were sufficient satisfied and impressed tasters to make the occasion a success, and his new regime in the kitchen was endorsed.

ALTHOUGH radical changes were made in the hospital kitchens, the actual time taken to do so was short – a matter of a few weeks – and as his new Soyer stoves hadn't yet been sent, he decided to join Florence Nightingale and her friends Mr and Mrs Bracebridge on a visit to the Crimea itself, as he thought that his work in the hospitals at Scutari would now carry on as he had planned.

He had had the approval of Lord William Paulet that each hospital should have a professional cook – he had brought four of his own staff with him – as well as a civilian assistant, and that they should be able to instruct the military orderlies, who would now be on regular assignment to the kitchens, and thus able to learn at least the rudiments of appropriate cooking.

Accordingly the party, which of course included the faithful T.G., set sail in the *Robert Lowe* for their voyage across the sea to the Crimean Peninsula. It was now May, and the weather was fine and sunny, and the journey itself must have been agreeable to those who had been so steadily involved with the difficult conditions in the hospital wards and kitchens.

The dinner on board must have been especially welcome too. "All bore testimony to the good fare provided by the captain, and exquisite pale sherry flowed in the glasses, in honour first of Her Majesty, then Miss Nightingale, next the ladies, and last not least, the Army and Navy. Some good old port, with a fine crust, properly decanted without shaking, was then introduced, with the inseparable and justly-famed Stilton cheese and fresh plain salad." Before that they had had the last decent piece of roast beef.

Another member of this party was a gentleman called Peter Morrison, usually referred to simply as P.M., and who was "a personage of no small importance in his own estimation", who had somehow attached himself to Soyer. Apparently he was courting some lady, who had decided that before she would give her hand he must prove himself in the service of his country, and more or less ordered him off to the Crimea. He became a target of amused scorn by Soyer and others as they soon discovered that when confronted with any danger his courage "oozed out at his fingers' ends".

On this particular voyage a looking glass had been damaged by one of the stewards who had lost his balance, his head having gone through the glass in such a way that it looked as if a cannon ball had shattered it. P.M. was very worried by this and the captain and his guests played up to the joke that it was indeed caused by a round shot, and poor P.M. spent the rest of the time bewailing the fact that he had not only come to the war in the first place, but that he had left the safety of Scutari, and matters became worse for him when they reached the harbour at Balaclava to find the words 'Cossack Bay' painted on the rocks, and some ill-favoured soldiers there. In fact they were Turks, but Soyer teased P.M. with the idea that they were Cossacks about to fire on them. "I shall not give them a chance," cried P.M. and off he bolted, and said later that he much regretted coming: "Oh, give me London and Red Lion Square, before any of your seats of war, for I see no fun in glory!"

A greater asset to their party was the drummer boy, Thomas, only twelve years old, who called himself Miss Nightingale's man, and was a devoted aide to her.

Soyer, too, became an increasingly devoted admirer of Miss Nightingale, and he gives a detailed description of her: "She is rather high in stature, fair in complexion and slim in person; her hair is brown, and is worn quite plain; her physiognomy is most pleasing; her eyes, of a blueish tint, speak volumes, and are always sparkling with intelligence; her mouth is small and well formed, while her lips act in unison, and make known the impression of her heart – one seems the reflex of the other. Her visage, as regards expression is very remarkable, and one can almost anticipate by her countenance what she is about to say . . . her dress is generally of a greyish or black tint; she wears a simple white cap, and often a rough apron. In a word her whole appearance is religiously simple and unsophisticated." When she went riding she wore "a genteel amazone, or riding-habit, and had quite a martial air".

Miss Nightingale and her party made the boat the *Robert Lowe* their lodgings, as it was almost impossible to find accommodation in Balaclava itself, and they set forth daily to inspect the various hospitals in the area, the nurse to the wards and the cook to the kitchens. It was Miss Nightingale's first visit to the Crimea as well as Soyer's, and there was much to see, do and plan. They made a journey to Sebastopol and found themselves getting uncomfortably near the firing – which of course terrified poor old P.M. even more. He made to run away, but was warned that if he did he might well be shot as a deserter, and reluctantly he remained with them. They were warned by the sentries not to go too far as they would be within shooting range, upon which Miss Nightingale said, "My good young man, more dead and wounded have passed through my hands than I hope you will ever see in the battlefield in the whole of your military career; believe me, I have no fear of death." They reached one of the batteries without incident, and managed to get a good view of the besieged city below them and Soyer begged a favour of Miss Nightingale, and asked her to climb on to one of the guns and sit upon it, which she did, and in a letter to his editor Delane, Russell wrote, "Soyer is here eating whatever he can get and obstinately deaf to all hints that he ought to come in time to cook the dinner. Miss Nightingale is very ill, poor soul. Soyer dragged her into a battery – the mortar battery out of fire – and put her on the stern of a gun with the elegant expression meant to be neat and well-turned – 'Voila! The Child of Peace had her breech on the breech of the Son of War!' "

This routine of visiting camps and hospitals continued for some weeks, and they moved to more spacious quarters on board another ship, the *London*. Soyer was anxious to meet Lord Raglan, the Commander-in-Chief of the British forces there, and whom he had met previously in London at the Reform Club. Eventually he did meet him along with the Turkish commander Omar Pasha, to whom he was introduced: "Monsieur Soyer is come to show our soldiers how to make the best of their rations, which I consider very kind of him." Raglan was shown plans and models of the kitchen that Soyer intended to set up in the Sanatorium Hospital at Balaclava, and his requests for help in making appropriate arrangements were granted, though it was easier to get permission than to get the work actually done, and the weather didn't help. Although it was summer the rain had been falling steadily and the whole area was a sea of mud. He took along a model of his camp stove which he hoped would soon be put into use, and he returned to his base on board the *London* in high spirits at the good reception he had had from Raglan.

However, as soon as he got on board he was greeted with the news that Florence Nightingale had been taken seriously ill with 'Crimean fever', and it was thought that she would not live. She was taken to the hospital and attended by her private nurse, Mrs Roberts, and the faithful Thomas, who was in deep distress. It was hardly surprising that she should have succumbed to the fever – she had been working so hard in such difficult conditions that she must have been quite exhausted, added to which the sodden weather must have made things even more unpleasant and difficult. Soyer had remarked to her only a few days before that she ought to have more suitable footwear than the thin boots she was wearing. However she gradually recovered from the fever, even though her health was never as good again, and she was urged to return to the safety and comparative comfort of Scutari.

Soyer also thought he ought to go back there too, but before doing so had to complete one or two other ideas that were in his mind. One of the difficulties the sick and wounded had to cope with was the very hard biscuit that served as bread. Many of them were in such a poor state that they could not manage to eat anything so hard, and although the bread at Scutari was good, that in the Crimea was not. It was made in Constantinople, was put on board ship before it was cold, shipped across the sea, and by the time it arrived was almost uneatable, especially for an invalid. There were no bakeries on the Crimea itself, so Soyer set about trying to establish them. He had a recipe for a flat cake of bread-biscuit which would keep well for months, and although quite dry it would soak well in liquids such as soup or tea, and was good and light. This was so well received that Russell mentioned its importance in his despatches home. Another refinement to the diet was to arrange for a firm in Paris to send out cakes of dried vegetables for use in soup, and packed in such a way that they would keep their quality and be regulated in quantity.

ALEXIS SOYER was not the only colourful civilian in the Crimea at that time. Mrs Seacole, "an old dame of jovial appearance, but a few shades darker than the white lily", had been running what became known as the British Hotel just outside Balaclava since the war began, and provided a welcome canteen for the soldiers, and other parts of the 'hotel' became a sort of London Club for the officers. Mary Seacole was a half-caste who had been brought up in Kingston, Jamaica, where her mother ran a boarding house patronised by naval and military families. She had a good idea of medicine and tropical diseases which she had learnt from her mother who was skilled in 'creole medical art', as well as being well trained in catering. Mrs Seacole was a popular, kind-hearted lady, known to her customers as Mother Seacole, and indeed she really looked after them in a very motherly way, often acting not only as unofficial nurse, but banker, letter-writer and confidante. She and Soyer each knew of the other's reputation and Soyer was glad to be taken to meet her, and they shared a bottle of champagne together. Unfortunately, on that occasion Soyer was riding a pony borrowed from Dr Hadley, the chief doctor at the Sanatorium (who had sent him off for the day saying that although he might lose the pony he *must not* lose the saddle), and when he came to leave Mrs Seacole neither the pony nor its saddle were anywhere in sight, and the Zouave to whom Soyer had entrusted the animal was seen to be holding quite a different beast. Soyer borrowed another pony from Mr Day, Mrs Seacole's partner, and though the pony was missing for several days it eventually reappeared, saddle intact, largely due to the efforts of Mrs Seacole who managed, by using her many contacts, to find it.

After Miss Nightingale gradually recovered from her fever and returned to Scutari, Soyer again accompanied her. He had achieved much at Balaclava – he had brought order and routine to the hospital kitchens, had organised bakeries to make wholesome and manageable bread, he had ordered proper rations of dried vegetables to replace the fresh ones that were usually delivered rotten. Now he wanted to return to Scutari to see that his orders there were being suitably carried out, and also he was impatiently awaiting the arrival of his patent camp stoves, and wanted to put them into action. Accordingly the party of Miss Nightingale, the Bracebridges; P.M. – still whimpering from fright at the sound of gunfire, were given the use of a yacht, which was thought to be more comfortable for the invalid to travel in, and they sailed for Scutari, which they reached in June 1855, only about four months since Soyer had left England.

He didn't intend to stay long in Scutari, just long enough to make sure that all his plans were working, as he had been told that his cook Julien (not to be confused with Jullien the musician) was leaving and returning to England. However, by this time the Sergeant whom he had had made supervisor to the soldier cooks, was doing very well and everything seemed in order. He returned to stay at Soyer House, which "was very cheerful, and rather elegant. It had the appearance of a large Swiss chalet. Vines grew round it; and if the windows were left open, branches of cherry and mulberry trees, loaded with ripe fruit, hung above one's head as one lay in bed." The horrors of the battlegrounds of Balaclava and Sebastopol in the Crimea must have seemed like another world. One evening the house began to shake vigorously "and the branches of the trees outside the windows entered very abruptly, and much farther than usual, sweeping off all the goblets and bottles from the tables, to our great astonishment, nearly upsetting us; when our friend P.M. exclaimed 'Who is shaking the house?' Julien, who had travelled much, replied "Don't be alarmed – it is only an earthquake.' " Whereupon P.M. bolted, collided with a servant bringing in some blazing punch so that he set himself alight, and disappeared until the next day.

Soyer's intention was to return briefly to the Crimea, then feeling his work was completed, to sail for England. His journey to the Crimea was delayed a few days, as Lord Raglan died, and he wished to pay respects to his remains on their journey back home, for he felt that Raglan had helped him so much in providing facilities for his kitchen work.

During this stay in Scutari he met the Selim Pasha, Governor of Asia Minor, who was gracious in the extreme, and, rather to Soyer's embarrassment and discomfort, insisted on taking and keeping hold of his hand while they walked several times up and down a large saloon, although "his pachaship" as Soyer called him, never once looked at his guest, and he only got his hand back when he was offered some coffee.

AT LAST the eagerly awaited field stoves arrived, and Soyer was impatient to get back to the Crimea to try them out. He realised that they would cost quite a bit to begin with, but was certain that the saving in fuel and transport would soon compensate for this. He taught the cooks at Scutari how to use them and being satisfied that they were competent, prepared to get to the Crimea at last, this time accompanied by a French Zouave called Bornet, who "was a capital shot and extraordinary good horseman; he could sing hundreds of songs, and very well too; ... among his other then unknown qualities, he was very quarrelsome; a great marauder à la Zouave; remarkably fond of the fair sex, in his martial way, running all over the camp after the heroic *cantinières*; and though never drunk, seldom sober, always ready to fight any one whom he thought wished to injure or speak ill of me. In fact, he was, much against my will, my bull-dog, and kept barking from morning till night." Soyer had a special uniform made for Bornet, and for himself adopted "an indescribable

Opening of Soyer's field kitchen before Sebastopol

costume", which was a white burnous with trousers with a blue and silver stripe down them, gold braid on his waistcoat and a red and white cap.

It must have been a colourful party altogether, with Soyer in his Oriental costume, Bornet in his new uniform, the faithful T.G., the gentleman of colour, clad all in white, and P.M. (who by now was becoming quite a brave man) "attired in nankeen, a very peculiar style".

Bornet proved quite a handful, dashing here and there, usually drinking too much himself, and getting his old comrades drunk as well, and when he heard that a big battle was expected went on the prowl at night and 'borrowed' some provisions, and begged to be allowed to go out and fight.

The field stoves were set up in the camp kitchens, and the men started using them at once, even before Soyer had instructed them in the correct use, but they were so efficient and so economical that not much instruction was needed. One of the great advantages of these stoves was that they would burn but twenty pounds of wood when being used for the rations for a hundred, whereas the previous apparatus would have used several hundredweight, which of course, would not only have been expensive in money, but also wasteful in time and transport.

The stoves were made of a material that needed no tinning, and were so simple in construction that there were no parts to go wrong. They had a large boiling copper with a chimney tall enough to carry the smoke above the cook's head, and until the lids were lifted no fire was visible, "a material point I had in view ... when used in the trenches". The particular ones that were used at first were rather too big, as they had been intended for use in the hospital kitchens, but it was easy to make smaller ones to the same pattern.

Soyer was justified in feeling proud of these stoves, which have remained in use until the present day. They were used by the Army in two world wars, with little or no modification, except in the actual fuel used, and are still used today by the National Voluntary Civil Aid Services when they need to provide cooking facilities in the open air. Apparently the Civil Aid workers make a kind of plum duff, which they put into bags and suspend over the soup or stew cooking in the boiler, so that a two-course meal is cooked at once. One of the workers told me that "it is a very obliging appliance and burns anything. We collect wood, usually damp, dry it against the boiler and start it off with paper". Soyer would be proud of them.

A grand opening ceremony was planned to show off the versatility of the stoves; a semi-circle of stoves was laid out, and "a common table made of a few boards, and garnished with soldiers' tin plates, iron forks and spoons, composed my open-air dining-room". Although they were designed primarily for cooking out of doors, Soyer makes the point that they could be used in huts too, which would mean that the place would be warmed through without the need for any other fire.

The menu for this opening feast was made from the regular rations, with the exception of soup made from ox-heads which had been specially ordered from the butcher, as they were usually thrown away. The rest of the meal was stewed fresh beef, Scotch hodgepodge of mutton, salt pork and beef with dumplings, and "this martial collation" was ended with a goblet of Marsala – not, I think, from the rations either, – and Soyer answered criticisms that he would spoil the soldiers who didn't need such food on campaign, by saying that it was " better to make a few good cooks out of an army than to have an army of bad cooks".

News of Soyer's activities were relayed to London, sometimes by the despatches of W.H. Russell, or by letters, both from Soyer himself and others, that appeared in *The Times*. *Punch* celebrated his success with a poem 'to be sung to the tune of the Minstrel Boy'.

The Cordon Bleu to the war is gone,
  In the ranks of death you'll find him.
His snow-white apron is girded on
  And his magic stove behind him.
'Army beef,' says the Cordon Bleu,
  Though a stupid bungler slays thee,
One skilful hand thy steaks shall stew,
  One artist's hand shall braise thee.'

Our cook went forth, and the foe in vain
  On his pots and pans did thunder.
He thicked thin gravy, he sauced the plain,
  And he sliced coarse lumps asunder.
And he cried, 'A cook can defy, you see,
  A Commissariat's knavery.
The soldier who saves a Nation free,
  Should have a ration savoury.'

Soyer doesn't dwell very greatly on the war itself, except to mention the constant stream of wounded soldiers who he met on the roads on their way to hospital, and after the Russians had retreated from Sebastopol he saw a train of wounded, some of them Russian, carried on mules, and a group of Russian prisoners all looking so young, not much above eighteen, and after the battle for Sebastopol was over, and "the curtain had fallen on this grand drama – all was repose. We then returned to quarters through the same mournful solitude, not having met a soul either going or returning. This dreariness impressed me with the idea of chaos, after the destruction of a world and its empires."

Bornet, his Zouave servant, continued to behave in an erratic way, disappearing without trace for a day or so, then returning usually half drunk and often with trophies he had acquired from goodness knows where. On one occasion, just

Dinner before Sebastopol

after the battle for Sebastopol where one of his friends was killed, he went off for the funeral, stayed away for two days and returned with an entirely new tent that had apparently belonged to a very senior officer. This time, to Soyer's surprise he came back sober, though he admitted that after the funeral of his comrade he "got boosy enough to make all the wine-sellers, and even old Father Bacchus himself, turn pale." But he slept it off and announced himself fit enough to dance upon a rope without a balance-pole.

Shortly after this Soyer, who had not been well for some while, fell really ill with the Crimean fever, but for some days didn't see a doctor, as he thought that he was just over-tired. The attack lasted some weeks, after which he was so changed in appearance that even some of his closer associates didn't recognise him, and the doctors had to order him back to Scutari to convalesce. When he got back to Scutari he even frightened his cooks, as they had been told that he was dead, "which I afterwards personally denied; but they did not think it was possible I could look so bad ... all consoled me by saying 'I fear you will never get over it, Monsieur Soyer' ... Nothing is less likely to restore a man when he is half dead than trying to persuade him that he must succumb. Thanks to my lucky star, I have deceived them all;

and some richly deserved it, as they had laid bets upon my chance, particularly my Zouave and another of my men." But only a few days later his health failed again. He dismissed Bornet, but on friendly terms so that the Zouave offered to come to London to serve him – that is if Soyer survived, which Bornet didn't think very likely. He went back to live in Soyer House, though he wrote that he "enjoyed the gay and interesting prospect for an invalid of the monster lugubrious cemetery, or Grand Champ des Morts, on one side, and the hospital on the other." He was laid up for about three months with fever and dysentery, though as soon as he could insisted that he must go back to the Crimea where a new consignment of stoves had arrived, and were waiting to be deployed. The doctor who had been attending him said cheerfully that if he must return to the Crimea he must take his tombstone with him.

Much of his recovery seemed to be due to the untiring efforts of a very young Dr Ambler, who changed the treatment of the first doctor to good effect, and Soyer eventually more or less recovered. Some months after this Ambler was taken ill himself, and Soyer returned his kindness with daily visits and dainty dishes suited to an invalid diet, until the doctor got well again, and they remained friends until Soyer's death.

When he reached the Crimea again he was allocated a hut, or, as he named it a 'villarette', on Cathcarts Hill, which he was to make his base. The stoves were all put to good use, and a routine was established by the cooks, and they were even persuaded to make good use of the fat from the salt meat rations, that hitherto had been thrown away as unusable. Soyer pointed out that if only they used more water with the salt meat the fat would be purified of salt, and he reckoned that he was able to save eight hundred pounds of good dripping a week this way.

By the middle of 1856 a peace treaty was signed with Russia, but although hostilities were over Soyer's work was not, as he was needed to instruct the soldiers in better cooking habits, as he assumed that, on their return to England, his stoves would still be used at Aldershot and other barracks – which turned out to be true.

He wrote: "War having ceased, the camp bore the appearance of a monster banqueting-hall. 'We have done fighting' said everyone, 'so let us terminate the campaign by feasting, lay down our victorious but murderous weapons, and pick up those more useful and restorative arms – the knife and fork' ... All appeared to have caught a giving-parties mania. You could scarcely meet a friend ... without being apostrophized by 'When will you dine with me?' as regularly as though it had been inserted in the order of the day." Everyone was relieved that such an unnecessary and bloody war was over, and it was not long before the Russians were on quite friendly terms with the Allies with whom they had been doing such fierce battles so recently, and senior officers were invited by General Lüders, the Russian commander, to a formal dinner at his camp, and there was an excellent and friendly reception when "the popping of the well-corked champagne had replaced the monstrous and unsociable voice of the cannon. The sparkling liquid, poured in tin pots or cups – anything but crystal champagne-glasses – seemed to unite all hearts."

This hospitality had, of course, to be returned, and in the middle of April 1856 Sir William Codrington, the Commander-in-Chief, gave a banquet to General Lüders, and asked Soyer for his help. This led to one of the most spectacular dishes: Soyer's Culinary Emblem of Peace, the *Macedoine Lüderaienne à l'Alexandre II*, the ingredients for which were published in one of Soyer's letters to *The Times*, and which consisted of 12 cases of preserved lobsters; cases of preserved lampreys; anchovies; sardines; caviar; oysters; turbot; pickled cucumbers; French beans; mushrooms; truffles; cockcombs and many other similarly exotic items. The only fresh ingredients were the turbot, some prawns, lettuces and eggs, everything else, including the oysters, being preserved or pickled. There was no dish big enough for this great extravaganza, so a lid from one of the field stoves had to be used, and the whole took two soldiers to carry to table. The final garnish was a wreath of olives, – he was teased by General Pellissier, the French commander, for not having stoned them – and small flags of the assembled nations.

Such jollities seemed to become the order of the day, and Soyer was kept busy with providing the food. It was summer and the weather hot, and for one of these banquets, this time for the Sardinian General della Marmora, he thought "that a new and well-iced beverage would be very acceptable during the hot weather", and devised the *Crimean Cup à la Marmora*, for which the recipe for 30 people was given as follows:

> Syrup of orgeat [which is almond flavoured] one quart; cognac brandy one pint; maraschino, half-a-pint; Jamaica rum half-a-pint; champagne two bottles; soda water, two bottles; sugar, six ounces; and four middling sized lemons.
>
> Thinly peal the lemons, and place the rind in a bowl with the sugar; macerate them well for a minute or two, in order to extract the flavour from the lemon. Next squeeze the juice of the lemons upon this, add two bottles of soda water, and stir well till the sugar is dissolved; pour in the syrup of orgeat, and whip the mixture with an egg-whisk, in order to whiten the composition. Then add the brandy, rum and maraschino; strain the whole into the punch-bowl, and just before serving add the champagne, which should be well iced. While adding the champagne, stir well with the ladle: this will render the cup creamy and mellow.

It would indeed have been very acceptable, I imagine. Soyer thought that he, too, ought to give a dinner in return for all the hospitality he had received, and he started to turn his little 'villarette' into a suitable 'Lucullusian temple'.

He obtained the services of half-a-dozen soldiers, who decorated the hut with green plants and bunches of flowers, and hung lights (which used ration fat as fuel) and flags outside. The whole looked very festive – except that the turf outside the hut had been burned brown by the sun which, he felt, would spoil the general effect. However, he went along to the camp theatre, got some green paint and set his soldiers to painting the grass. He said that this was so cleverly done that it even fooled the horses tethered nearby, who wanted to get into the "beautiful and succulent looking field." Everything went well, even though one of the lamps nearly set the house on fire; the guests were happy and *punch à la Marmora* was produced, songs were sung, and the last guests didn't leave until five in the morning.

This was more or less the end of his time in the Crimea though he did manage to make a visit to Odessa, in company with W.H. Russell among others. The hospitals were of course still much in use, and Miss Nightingale was very busy in both Balaclava and Scutari. She was duly impressed by the simplicity and durability of the stoves, and although in her letters she admits that some of the soldiers didn't like Soyer's cooking, she herself believed in him, even though she had heard him described as a 'humbug' for leaving his work half-done and going on too quickly to something else. But she wrote a testimonial to 'his essential usefulness' in restoring order and converting the issued rations into agreeable food. During one of her journeys to the various hospitals Miss Nightingale had an accident, when the mule-cart in which she was travelling overturned. She was not hurt though one of the nurses accompanying her was injured quite badly. As a result of this incident one of the officers gave her a carriage which was more stable and comfortable, and she used this transport for the rest of her stay. At the end of his time in the Crimea Soyer found that this carriage was up for sale, among a job lot of carts, harness and so on, and was to be bought by some Tartar jews, so bought it, as he thought of it as "a precious relic for present and future generations", had it shipped back to England at his own expense, and until recently it has been on view at St Thomas's Hospital in London, which has been so closely associated with Florence Nightingale. Unfortunately it seems that boisterous medical students didn't treat it with due respect and it has now been transferred to the headquarters of the Queen Alexandra Nurses at Camberley, but a model of it is at the Florence Nightingale Museum at St Thomas's.

SOYER made his farewells, particularly to Mrs Seacole and her beautiful daughter, and all at the hospitals, and prepared for the journey back to England, in company with a great many others who felt that their work was now done. Just before the ship sailed a young Russian boy, ragged and bruised, was discovered on board. He was interrogated and told the company that he was an orphaned serf of Prince Meshersky, and that his name was Daniel Maximovitch Chimachenka. He had been ill-treated since the Prince had been away at the war, had escaped and now hoped that the English would be kind to him. He was only twelve. Soyer took him under his wing, sent him at the first opportunity to a Turkish bath which "removed two or three coats of dirt from his skin", clothed him and took him back to London, where he became a devoted servant. Soyer had been away from England for the best part of two years. He had achieved much in the things he had set out to do, but his lasting memorial is the field stove, which has long outlasted him.

The war in the Crimea was one of incompetence, bravery – it was for this war that the Victoria Cross was created – and sacrifice. Its legacy lives on, not only for the romanticised Charge of the Light Brigade, but in more everyday ways. It is to this war that we owe the Balaclava helmet, the Cardigan, the Raglan sleeve – and Soyer's field stove, and the lasting effects of his kitchen organisation.

IX
Farewell, Soyer

After Soyer had returned to London – much altered in appearance, and his health uncertain – his work for the army was not over. Miss Nightingale wrote a report to the Royal Commission on the Sanitary Condition of the Army, as she was so concerned with the arrangements for the health and diet of the soldiers who, she wrote, "enlist to death in the barracks". The Government had been made uncomfortably aware of the deficiencies in these matters as had the public, and everyone realised that Miss Nightingale was not the kind of person to let a matter of such importance drop, and eventually it was agreed that improvements would be made.

Experts in every field were called upon, and Soyer was asked to undertake the redesigning and restructuring of the army kitchens, and he based his first efforts on a new model kitchen at Wellington Barracks.

Punch described him as "the Soldiers' Friend":

> *The soldier tired of tough boiled beef,*
> *Fed worse than any rogue or thief,*
>   *Henceforth shall better fare:*
> *On fried, and stewed, and roast and boiled,*
> *And vegetables, cooked, not spoiled,*
>   *By Soyer's art and care.*

From beef to mutton he shall range,
And then to ox-heart have a change,
  Or make his varied meal,
On liver of the calf, whereto,
Shall bacon join, as it should do,
  With anything of veal.

Cabbage, potatoes, and what not,
The soldier in the charmed pot,
  Of Soyer's new device,
In divers modes can cook, with ease,
Turnips and carrots, beans and peas,
  And dumplings, pudding, rice.

He produced a booklet, *Instructions to Military Hospital Cooks*, with suitable recipes, which was adopted by all the military hospitals, and remembering the badly preserved food in the Navy that had caused such a scandal a year or so earlier, he made suggestions for improving the canning processes, and produced designs for a mobile cooking apparatus to be used for any army on the move, and he lectured to the United Service Institution on the subject.

He worked as hard as his failing health would allow – not only had he never really recovered from the fevers he had suffered in the Crimea, but he had had a nasty fall from a horse which had shaken him badly, – and by the early part of 1858 he was in considerable discomfort. Perhaps he realised that he had not long to live and worked desperately hard to get his Wellington Barracks project finished. This he succeeded in doing, and the kitchens were opened successfully in July 1858. He died on 5th August, just a month later, and was buried beside his beloved Emma at Kensal Green.

There were tributes and obituaries, both public and private – Miss Nightingale wrote that "His death is a great disaster . . . he has no successor."

His friend George Augustus Sala, who was very fond of him, while accepting that his faults were many and various, wrote, "Soyer, indeed, was continually inventing something, and his not altogether unreasonable anxiety that due publicity should be attained by his inventions led to his being very frequently disparaged as a charlatan.

"That there may have been a slight spice of the *poseur* in his composition it would be idle to deny; but his foible in this direction was a perfectly harmless one, and it was more than compensated by the real talent of the man, by his great capacity for organisation, and by the manliness, simplicity, and uprightness of his character ... He was only a cook; but I shall always cherish the remembrance of my friendship with him, not only because I sincerely admired his character, but because I consider him to have been a thoroughly capable and refined culinary artist."

Sala also pointed out that "no honorific distinction was conferred on him by the British Government, or that any kind of pension or annuity was settled on him," and *Punch*, some time earlier when Soyer was still in the Crimea, asked: "But how will the British Government – at length so wide awake to merit – distinguish the man who is the benefactor of the sick and wounded British soldier!" and goes on to list all the other people who have been honoured, some way or another. "If, however, a Lord Mayor be turned into a Baronet for supplying an Emperor with luncheon, it follows that a wizard cook should be correspondingly honoured for solacing and strengthening the vitals of a whole army ... we do not see how Soyer can escape an Earldom at least ... The Earl of Scutari!"

But his honours lie in the work that he left behind him, and no public recognition was given to him. After all ... he was only a cook.

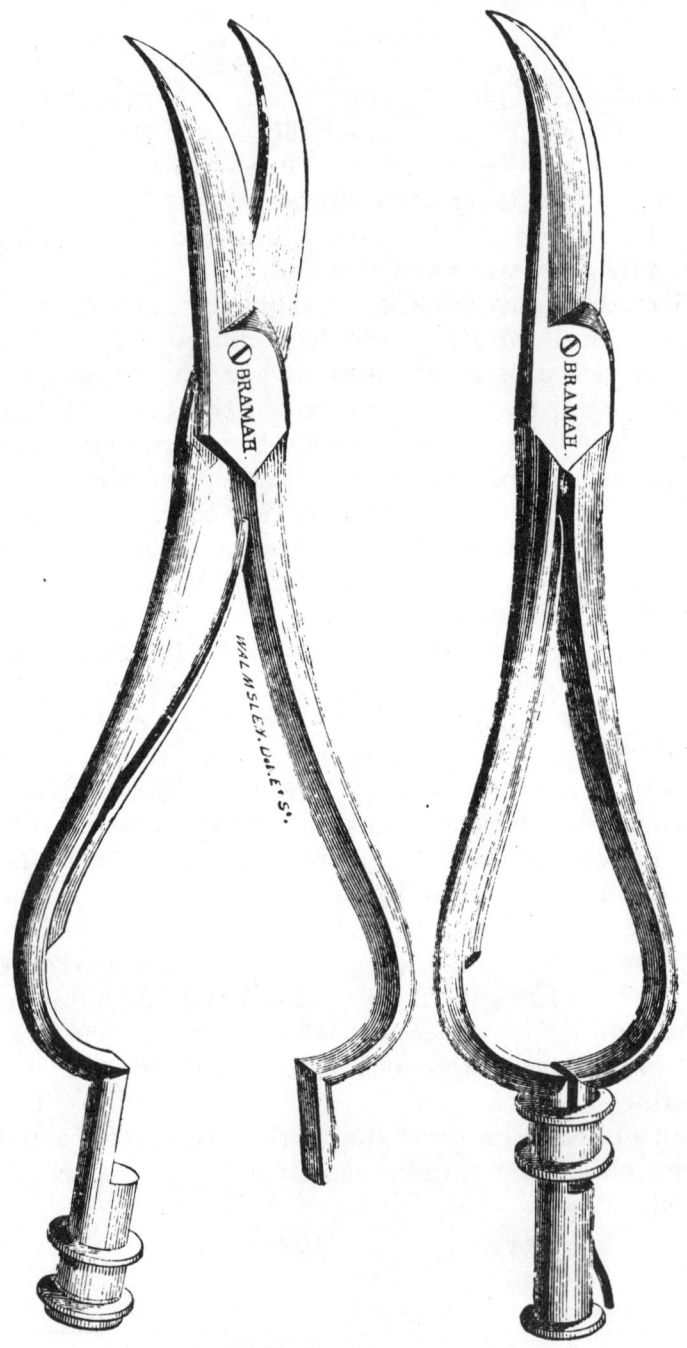

Tendon separators

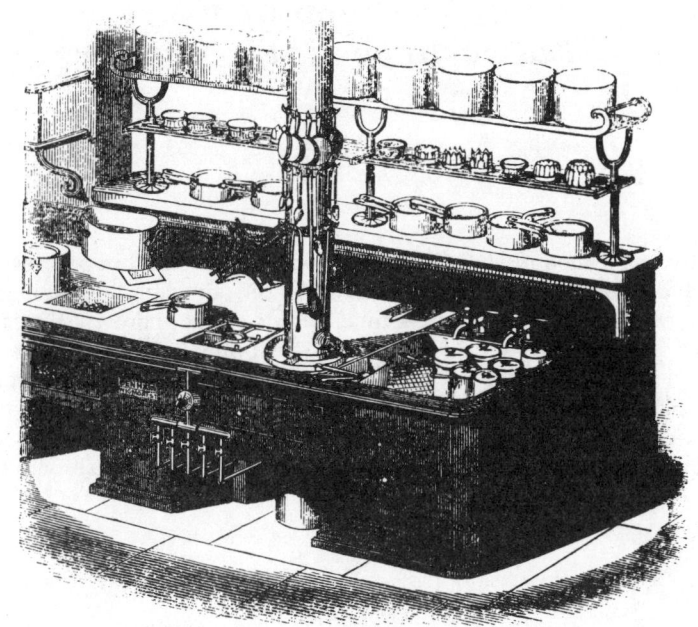

Gas stove, etc.

Recipes

There follows a very short selection from two of Soyer's books. The first part is taken from *The Gastronomic Regenerator*, which contains recipes that, on the whole, are more suited to the large household or establishment. I have tried to choose those that are either typical of his style of writing, or which can be adapted for use today.

The second selection comes from *The Modern Housewife*, with recipes that were designed, as the title indicated, for the more modest, middle-class home.

It is, of necessity, an arbitrary selection; *The Gastronomic Regenerator* alone contains about fifteen hundred recipes.

Selections from
The Gastronomic Regenerator

30
Sauce à l'Italienne

Put two tablespoonfuls of chopped onions and one of chopped eschalots in a stewpan with three tablespoons of salad oil, stir them ten minutes over a sharp fire; then add a wine-glassful of sherry, a pint of brown sauce and half a pint of consommé, set it over a sharp fire until it boils, then place it at the corner, let it simmer ten minutes, skim off all the oil which it will throw up, then place it over the fire, stir with a spoon, reducing it until it adheres to the back of it, then add a teaspoonful of chopped parsley, a tablespoonful of chopped mushrooms, a little sugar, salt if required, and finish with the juice of half a lemon.

106
Epinard au Jus

Pick all the stalks off and wash the spinach very clean in several waters, have ready a large stewpan of boiling water, in which you have put a handful of salt, put in the spinach, and let it boil as quickly as possible about twenty minutes; when quite tender put it into a colander and press the water out until there is none remaining, then chop it very fine; put one pound of spinach into a stewpan with a quarter of a pound of butter, stir it with a wooden spoon over a moderate fire until the butter is melted; then add a little flour, eight tablespoonfuls of brown sauce, half a teaspoonful of salt, half ditto of sugar, a little white pepper, and very small quantity of grated nutmeg; a little glaze may be added; finish with two ounces of fresh butter.

No receipt has been included for a Brown Sauce, as it is assumed readers will be familiar with it. In effect it is made the same way as a white sauce, except that the roux is cooked until it is brown, and the liquid is a well flavoured meat stock instead of milk.

216
Brill au Naturel

This fish though not so much thought of as turbot is very delicate eating, and being cheaper may be more freely used for fillets, &c., and may be recommended cooked in the following ways: – Boil a brill as you would a turbot, but the flesh being softer than that fish you put it in boiling water; if the fish weighs from four to five pounds, put it into six quarts of water in which there is one pound of salt, draw the kettle to the corner of the fire and let it simmer for half an hour, try whether it is done as you would a turbot, drain it and dish it on a napkin; garnish with parsley, and serve with shrimp sauce.

217
Brill à la Purée de Câpres

Take a very fresh fish, and an hour before cooking rub a good handful of salt on it, then boil it as before, dish it without a napkin, and have ready the following sauce: put a pint and a half of melted butter into a stewpan, then have ready prepared three tablespoonfuls of capers, and two of gherkins, with a little boiled spinach pounded in a mortar with four ounces of fresh butter, and passed through a hair sieve, and when the melted butter is nearly boiling stir it quickly into it; finish it with a little essence of anchovy, a little cayenne pepper, and a little sugar, and pour over the fish when ready to serve. The butter requires to lay upon ice until quite hard.

253
Sole à la Polonaise

Trim a fine sole and make an incision down the back clearing the meat from the bone, then melt two ounces of butter, and mix with it a teaspoonful of chopped eschalots, one of chopped mushrooms, one of chopped parsley, and a glass of sherry; put the sole in a dish and pour the butter, etc., over it, sprinkle a few breadcrumbs on it and put it in the oven twenty minutes or half an hour; when done pour a little anchovy sauce over it, and brown it lightly with the salamander.

A salamander was a metal-ended implement, heated in the fire and then held over the dish to brown the food. A grill produces the same result now.

689
Côtelettes de Veau en Papillote

Cut six small veal côtelettes, do not lard them, put six tablespoonfuls of oil in a sauté-pan, in which fry the côtelettes; when done pour off a little of the oil, put four tablespoonfuls of chopped onions, one of chopped parsley, one of chopped mushrooms, and twenty of brown sauce seasoned rather high, moisten with a little stock and simmer altogether twenty minutes, place the côtelettes on a dish in the sauce to get cold, cut six pieces of paper in the shape of hearts, oil them, and put a côtelette in each with as much of the sauce as possible around, fold each one up, plaiting it at the edges, broil them twenty minutes over a slow fire, and dress them in a circle on your dish without removing the papers.

729
Rognons de Mouton Sauté au Vin de Champagne

Skin eight kidneys and cut them into thin slices, put an ounce of butter in a stewpan, place it over the fire, and when the butter begins to brown throw in the kidneys, stir round with a wooden spoon and when they become firm add a small tablespoon of flour, mix well, add two wine-glasses of champagne with two of white broth and twenty blanched mushrooms; let all boil very gently a few minutes, season with the juice of half a lemon, a little pepper, salt, and chopped parsley; pour them out on your dish and serve. The sauce requires to be rather thick, sherry or hock may be used instead of champagne.

784
Hashed Venison

The remains of a haunch of venison when cold is much thought of as hash, under which humble name it makes its appearance amongst the most sumptuous dishes, and is a great favourite with epicures, but if no fat remains do not attempt to dress it; but a good haunch well-carved will supply sufficient fat to hash the remainder.

Put a quart of good brown sauce in a stewpan with a pint of consommé, a piece of glaze, and a good bunch of parsley, let reduce to a good demi-glace, skim, then have as much venison as you require cut in thin slices, the fat thicker than the lean, put it into the sauce, season with pepper and salt, put it over a sharp fire to get hot as quick as possible, but do not let it boil or it would get hard and become very greasy, serve as hot as possible, with red currant jelly separate, make only sufficient for one entrée.

RECIPES

304
Mackerel à la Maître d'Hôtel

Fillet your mackerel as you would whitings by passing the knife down the backbone, lay your fillets in a buttered sauté-pan (the skin side upwards), with two tablespoonfuls of oil, two of port wine, and season with a little pepper and salt; place them over a sharp fire ten minutes, then turn them and place them over again five minutes longer, or till they are done, take them out, cut each fillet in halves, and dish them round on a dish without a napkin; then put twelve tablespoonfuls of brown sauce into the sauté-pan, let it boil five minutes, then add a teaspoonful of chopped mushrooms, half ditto of chopped parsley, a little lemon juice, and a small quantity of sugar; chop the roe of the mackerel and put in the sauce, let it simmer five minutes, pour it over the fillets, cover them lightly with breadcrumbs, brown lightly with the salamander and serve very hot. The sauce must not be too thick.

482
Necks of Mutton à la Légumière

Cut off the scrags and take the chine bones from two necks of mutton, lard the lean parts with lardons of fat bacon about three inches long, roast them in vegetables as for fillet of beef; when done, dress them on a dish, placing fillet to fillet, so as to form a saddle; fill up the crevice between them with mashed potatoes, upon which dress small pieces of cauliflower and small bunches of asparagus, or Brussels sprouts; make a border of mashed potatoes round the mutton, upon which dress some onions, with pieces of carrots and turnips stewed, place four onions at each end of the dish, and stick a fine head of asparagus in each; glaze the mutton, and pour a demi-glace over the vegetables.

498
Boiled Leg of Lamb and Spinach

Boil a leg of lamb quite plain, which will take from an hour and a quarter to an hour and a half (add a little milk to the water you boil it in), have ready dressed sufficient spinach to cover the bottom of the dish an inch and a half in thickness, dress the lamb upon it, and serve; to dress spinach, see No. 106.

817
Filets de Volaille aux Concombres

Fillet three fowls as usual, place them in a sauté-pan with butter, season and put by until ready; have two fine cucumbers cut in pieces three inches in length, split each piece in halves, take out the seeds and peel so as not to leave a mark of green upon it, trim each piece as near the size and shape of the fillets as possible, blanch them three minutes in boiling water with salt, drain them on a sieve, put them in a sauté-pan with a little sugar and some good white stock, set them on the fire till the cucumber is tender and the stock has reduced to demi-glace, then sauté your fillets, and dress upon a small border of mashed potatoes alternately with a piece of the cucumber, add the remainder of the cucumber and the demi-glace to a demi-purée of cucumbers (but keep it white), with which sauce over and serve. The cucumbers must be the best for this purpose and fresh, or you will not be able to succeed.

1038
Salade de Grouse à la Soyer

Make a very thin border of fresh butter upon a convenient-sized dish, upon which stand a very elevated border of hard-boiled eggs (by cutting a piece off the bottoms when quite cold and cutting each one into four length wise), fill the centre with some nice fresh salad, and ornament the eggs with fillets of anchovies, beetroot, gherkins, &c., according to taste; you have previously roasted three grouse rather underdone; when quite cold cut them into neat pieces, that is, into legs, wings, part of the backs, and each breast into six slices, then have ready the following sauce: put two tablespoonfuls of finely chopped eschalots in a basin, with two tablespoonfuls of powdered sugar, the yolks of two eggs, two tablespoonfuls of chopped tarragon and chervil, a saltspoonful of white pepper, and two of salt, with which mix by degrees twelve tablespoonfuls of salad oil and three of Chili vinegar; mix well together and place it upon the ice; when ready to serve whip half a pint of cream rather stiff, which add to the sauce, pour a little over the salad, upon which lay some of the worst pieces of grouse, over which put more sauce, proceeding in like manner to the top, dressing them pyramidically. When it is for the flanc of a large dinner I only use the fillets, roasting four or five grouse instead of three, and when you have dressed three parts of the pieces of grouse upon the salad, build a second row of eggs upon it, having formed a level with the pieces for that purpose, and terminate exactly as the design represents. I must observe that the salad is better adapted for gentlemen than ladies, though if less eschalot were used it might also meet their approbation.

RECIPES

The first time I served a salad of the above description after inventing it was in a dinner which I dressed for some noblemen and gentlemen who had made a wager as to which could send the best dinner, myself or the artiste at a celebrated establishment in Paris, where they had previously dined; my first course being full of novelty, gained the approbation of the whole party, but the salad created such an unexpected effect that I was sent for, and had the honour of sitting at the table for an hour with them and over several rosades of exquisite Laffitte; the salad was christened à la Soyer by General Sir Alexander Duff, who presided over the noble party.

1051
Salade de Filets de Soles

Fillet two or three soles, then well butter a sauté-pan, lay in your fillets, which season with a little white pepper, salt, chopped parsley, and the juice of a lemon, place them over a slow fire, and when half done turn them over (they must be kept quite white), when done lay them flat upon a dish with another dish upon them till cold; cut each fillet in halves, trim them of nice shapes, and put them in a basin with a little chopped tarragon and chervil, chopped eschalots, pepper and salt; then dress a salad as directed (No. 1038), dress the fillets in crown upon the salad, and sauce over with a good mayonnaise sauce.

1069
Cauliflowers and Broccoli

Both vegetables are very excellent and universally employed; they require great particularity in cleaning; the best way is to throw plenty of salt over them and put them in cold water till ready to cook, boil them in salt and water till tender, but not too much done or they will not hold together; the heads should not be too large, and the best are close and firm; when done dress some nice green Brussels sprouts upon a border of mashed potatoes with the cauliflowers in the centre, mix nearly half a pint of good white sauce, with the same quantity of melted butter, and when hot add a liaison of one yolk of egg mixed with two spoonfuls of cream; sauce over and serve; they may also be served with a sauce à la maître d'hôtel.

1257
Bavaroise aux Abricots

Take twelve ripe fleshy apricots, cut them in halves, stone them, and put them into a preserving-pan with half a pound of sugar, the juice of two lemons, and an ounce of isinglass, dissolved in a little water, stew them till quite tender, then rub them through a tammie, put them in a basin when cold, stir it upon the ice, and when upon the point of setting add a pint of cream well whipped, and pour into your mould.

1280
Pommes à la Trianon

Put four ounces of ground rice in a stewpan, with a pint and a quarter of milk and two ounces of butter, stir until boiling, then add the rind of a lemon cut very thin, let simmer over a slow fire until the rice is done and becomes rather thick, when take out the lemon-peel and add a quarter of a pound of powdered sugar and the yolks of eight eggs, stir again over the fire until the eggs are set, and put it out upon a dish to get cold, then turn twelve golden pippin apples, taking off the rind without leaving the mark of your knife, having previously with a long vegetable cutter taken out the cores, rub the apples with lemon-juice and stew them in a thick syrup (made with three quarters of a pound of sugar boiled with half a pint of water and the juice of a lemon), stew them until tender, but keep them whole, peel and quarter three oranges, which (after having taken out the apples) just give a boil up in the syrup, then dress the rice in a pyramid in the centre of your dish, surrounded with the apples interspersed with the quarters of oranges, and pour the syrup over when ready to serve.

1355
Petites Fondues (en Caisse) au Stilton

Put six ounces of butter and half a pound of flour in a stewpan, rub well together with a wooden spoon, then add a quart of warm milk, stir over the fire a quarter of an hour, then add the yolks of eight eggs, three quarters of a pound of grated Parmesan, and half a pound of Stilton cheese in small dice, season rather highly with pepper, salt, and cayenne, add the white of the eggs whipped very stiff, which stir in lightly; have a dozen and a half of small paper cases, fill each one three parts full, place them in a moderate oven, bake about twenty minutes; when done dress them upon a napkin on your dish, and serve very hot.

Selected Recipes from
The Modern Housewife

40
Black Puddings, Broiled

Make about six or eight incisions through the skin with a knife, slantwise, on each side of the pudding; put it on the gridiron for about eight minutes, over rather a brisk fire; turn it four times in that space of time, and serve broiling hot.

I should recommend those who are fond of black puddings to partake of no other beverage than tea or coffee, as cocoa or chocolate would be a clog to the stomach. In France they partake of white wine for breakfast, which accounts for the great consumption of black pudding. Now really this is a very favourite dish with epicures, but I never recommend it to a delicate stomach.

Soyer's vegetable drainer

146
Ravigote Sauce

Put in a stewpan one middle-sized onion sliced, with a little carrot, a little thyme, bay-leaf, one clove, a little mace, a little scraped horseradish, a little butter, fry a few minutes, then add three teaspoonfuls of vinegar, ten tablespoonfuls of brown sauce, four of broth; when boiling, skim, add a tablespoonful of currant jelly: when melted, pass all through a tammie, and serve with any kind of meat or poultry: with hare or venison it is excellent.

148
Orange Sauce for Game

Peel half an orange, removing all the pith; cut it into slices, and then in fillets; put them in a gill of water to boil for two minutes; drain them on a sieve, throwing the water away; place in the stewpan two spoonfuls of demi-glaze, or ten of broth; and, when boiling, add the orange, a little sugar, simmer ten minutes, skim, and serve. The juice of half an orange is an improvement. This is served with ducklings and water-fowl: those that like may add cayenne and mustard.

151
Palestine Soup, or Purée of Artichokes

Have a quarter of a pound of lean bacon or ham, as also an onion, a turnip, and a little celery, cut the whole into small thin slices, and put them into a stewpan, with four ounces of butter; place them over a sharp fire, keeping them stirred, about twenty minutes, or until forming a whitish glaze at the bottom; then have ready washed, peeled, and cut into thin slices, about twelve artichokes, which put into the stewpan with a pint of broth or water, and stew until quite tender, then mix in two tablespoonfuls of flour quite smoothly, add two quarts of stock and half a pint of milk; keep it constantly stirred until boiling; season with a teaspoonful of salt, and two of sugar, then rub it through a tammie, place it again in a stewpan; let it boil five minutes, keeping it well skimmed, and serve with very small croutons of bread (fried in butter, and dried upon a cloth) in the tureen; a gill of cream, stirred in at the moment of serving, is a great improvement, although it may be omitted.

RECIPES

218
Crecy `a la Reine, or Purée of White Carrot

Procure six large white Belgian carrots, scrape them, and then cut into very thin slices; put them into a stewpan with a quarter of a pound of butter, the same of lean bacon or ham, a large onion and turnip, and a very white head of celery, all cut into thin slices, and proceed as for Palestine Soup.

246
Whiting au Gratin

Put a good spoonful of chopped onions upon a strong earthen dish, with a glass of wine, season the whiting with a little pepper and salt, put it in the dish, sprinkle some chopped parsley and chopped mushrooms over, and pour over half a pint of anchovy sauce, over which sprinkle some brown breadcrumbs, grated from the crust of bread, place it in a warm oven half an hour; it requires to be nicely browned; serve upon the dish you have cooked it in.

253
Herrings Broiled, Sauce Dijon

The delicacy of these fish prevents their being dressed in any other way than boiled or broiled; they certainly can be bread-crumbed and fried, but scarcely any person would like them; I prefer them dressed in the following way: wipe them well with a cloth, and cut three incisions slant-wise upon each side, dip them in flour, and broil slowly over a moderate fire; when done, sprinkle a little salt over, dress them upon a napkin, garnish with parsley, and serve the following sauce in a boat: put eight tablespoonfuls of melted butter in a stewpan, with two of French mustard,* or one of English, an ounce of fresh butter, and a little pepper and salt; when upon the point of boiling, serve.

*Dijon is the town in France so celebrated for its mustard.

273
Trout à la Twickenham

When you have cleaned your trout, put them into a kettle of boiling water, to which you have added a good handful of salt, and a wine-glassful of vinegar; boil gently about twenty minutes, or according to their size, dress upon a napkin, and serve melted butter, into which you have put a tablespoonful of chopped gherkins, two sprigs of chopped parsley, salt and pepper, in a boat.

The remains of trout, salmon, or mackerel, are excellent pickled: put three onions in slices in a stewpan, with two ounces of butter, one turnip, a bouquet of parsley, thyme, and bay-leaf, pass them five minutes over the fire, add a pint of water and a pint of vinegar, two teaspoonfuls of salt and one of pepper, boil until the onions are tender, then strain it through a sieve over the fish; it will keep some time if required, and then do to pickle more fish by boiling over again.

316
To Pot Beef

If there are of the remains of ribs of beef, take all the meat from the bones, remove the skin, and separate the fat from the meat, mince the meat into small pieces, melt the fat and strain it. To one pound of meat cut up a small onion about one inch in diameter into small pieces, place it in a frying-pan with a little fat, and fry it; when brown throw in the meat, and give it a turn or two, remove it, and place it in a mortar, pound it well, adding whilst pounding, five ounces of fat, or if not fat enough, fresh butter, to every pound of meat, and a little cayenne, half a teaspoonful of grated mace, ditto nutmeg; when well mixed, place it in pots, and cover it over with clarified butter and paper; keep it in a dry place.
Poultry and game may be done in the same way, using butter instead of fat.

357
Breast of Lamb Braised, Broiled

Saw off the breast from the ribs of lamb, leaving the neck of sufficient size to roast, or for cutlets; then put two onions, half a carrot, and the same of turnip, cut into thin slices, in a stewpan with two bay-leaves, a few sprigs of parsley and thyme, half an ounce of salt, and three pints of water; lay in the breast, which let simmer until tender, and the bones leave with facility; take it from the stewpan, pull out all the bones, and press it between two dishes; when cold, season with a little salt and pepper, egg and breadcrumb it lightly over, and broil gently (over a moderate fire) of a nice yellowish colour, turning it very carefully; when sufficiently browned upon one side, serve with plain gravy in the dish, and mint sauce separately, or with stewed peas or any other vegetable sauce; tomato sauce is likewise very good served with it.

365
Loin or Neck of Pork à la Piemontaise

The neck or loin must be plain roasted; peel and cut four onions in dice, put them into a stewpan, with two ounces of butter, stir over the fire until rather brown, then add a tablespoonful of flour, mix well, add a good pint of broth, if any, or water, with an ounce of glaze, boil ten minutes, add two tablespoonfuls of French mustard, with a little pepper, salt, and sugar, pour the sauce upon the dish, and dress your joint upon it, serve with a little apple sauce separate in a boat.

386
Capon or Poulard à l'Estragon

I have been told many fanciful epicures idolize this dish. The bird should be trussed for boiling. Rub the breast with half a lemon, tie over it some thin slices of bacon, cover the bottom of a small stewpan with this slices of the same, and a few trimmings of either beef, veal, or lamb, two onions, a little carrot, turnip and celery, two bay-leaves, one sprig of thyme, a glass of sherry, two quarts of water, season lightly with salt, pepper, and nutmeg, simmer about one hour and a quarter, keeping continually a little fire on the lid, strain three parts of the gravy into a small basin, skim off the fat, and pass through a tammie into a small stewpan, add a drop of gravy or colouring to give it a nice brown colour, boil a few minutes longer, and take about forty tarragon leaves; wash, and put it in the boiling gravy, with a tablespoonful of good French vinegar, and pour over the capon when you serve it; it is an improvement to clarify the gravy. All kinds of fowls and chickens are continually cooked in this manner in France. They are also served with rice.

403
Ducks à l'Aubergiste (or Tavern-keepers' fashion)

Truss one or two ducks with the legs turned inside, put them into a stewpan with a quarter of a pound of butter; place them over a slow fire, turning round occasionally, until they have taken a nice brown colour, add two spoonfuls of flour, mix well with them, add a quart of water, with half a tablespoonful of salt and sugar, let simmer gently until the ducks are done (but adding forty button onions well peeled as soon as it begins to boil), keep hot; peel and cut ten turnips in slices, fry them in a frying-pan in butter, drain upon a cloth, put them into the sauce, and stew until quite tender; dress the ducks upon your dish, skim the fat from the sauce, which has attained a consistency, add some fresh mushrooms, pour round the ducks, and serve.

423
Bubble and Squeak

I am certain you must know, as well as myself, our hereditary dish called bubble and squeak; but, like the preparation of other things, there is a good way and a bad; and, as you prefer the former to the latter, proceed as follows: boil a few greens, or a savoy cabbage (which has been previously well washed) in plain water until tender, which then drain quite dry in a colander or sieve, put it upon a trencher, and chop it rather fine with a knife, then for a pound of salt beef you have in slices, put nearly a quarter of a pound of butter into a frying-pan, in which sauté the beef gently but not too dry; when done, keep it hot, put the cabbage in the frying-pan, season with a little salt and pepper, and when hot through, dress it upon a dish, lay the beef over, and serve. Endive or large cabbage-lettuces may be used instead of cabbage, but care must be taken to drain off all the water.

424
Stewed Beef or Rump Steak

Have a steak weighing two pounds, and an inch and a half in thickness, then put two ounces of butter at the bottom of a stewpan, when melted lay in the steak, with a quarter of a pound of lean bacon cut into very small square pieces, place the stewpan over the fire, turning the steak over occasionally until a little browned, when lay it out upon a dish, then add a tablespoonful of flour to the butter in the stewpan, which continue stirring over the fire, until forming a brownish roux; then again lay in the steak, add a pint of water, with a glass of sherry if handy, and a little pepper, salt, and a bay-leaf, let simmer slowly for one hour, skim off all the fat, and add twenty button onions, let it again simmer until the onions are very tender, as likewise the steak, which dress upon a dish, take the onions and bacon out with a colander-spoon, and lay them upon the steak, pour the sauce round, and serve. This slow process must not alarm you, as it is indispensable.

RECIPES

433
A Family French Salad for the Summer

I can assure you that when in France, during the hot weather, I used to enjoy the following salads immensely, having them usually twice a week for my dinner; they are not only wholesome, but cheap and quickly done. Cut up a pound of cold beef into thin slices, which put into a salad-bowl, with about half a pound of white fresh lettuce, cut into pieces similar to the beef, season over with a good teaspoonful of salt, half that quantity of pepper, two spoonfuls of vinegar, and five of good salad oil, stir all together lightly with a fork and spoon, and when well mixed it is ready to serve.

For a change, cabbage-lettuce may be used, or, if in season, a little endive (well washed), or a little celery, or a few gherkins; also, to vary the seasoning, a little chopped tarragon and chervil, chopped eschalots, or a little scraped garlic, if approved of, but all in proportion, and used with moderation. White haricot beans are also excellent with it. Remains of cold veal, mutton, or lamb, may be dressed the same way.

503
Fricassee of Fowl

Divide a fowl into eight pieces, wash it well, put the pieces into a stewpan, and cover with boiling water, season with a teaspoonful of salt, a little pepper, a good bouquet of parsley, four cloves, and a blade of mace; let it boil twenty minutes; pass the stock through a sieve into a basin; take out the pieces of fowl, trim nicely, then put into another stewpan two ounces of butter, with which mix a good spoonful of flour, moisten with stock, put in the pieces of fowl, stir occasionally until boiling, skim well, add twenty button onions, let simmer until the onions are tender, when add a gill of cream, with which you have mixed the yolks of two eggs, stir it quickly over the fire, but do not let it boil; take out the pieces, dress in form of pyramid upon the dish, and serve.

If you require to warm up the remainder of the above, put it into a basin, which stand in a stewpan in which you have placed a little water, put the cover over, and let it boil gently, by which means the contents of the basin will get warm without turning the sauce; when hot, dish up and serve. The same plan ought to be adopted to warm up any remains of dishes in which a liaison has been introduced; it prevents its turning, which is unavoidable in any other.

569
Pheasant Stewed with Cabbage

The following is an excellent method for dressing a pheasant which should prove to be rather old, although a young one would be preferable. Procure a large savoy cabbage, which cut into quarters, and well wash in salt and water, after which boil it five minutes in plain water, then drain it quite dry, cut off the stalk, season rather highly with pepper and salt, have ready a middling-sized onion, and half a pound of streaky bacon, which, with the cabbage, put into a stewpan, covering the whole with a little good broth; let it simmer at the corner of the fire three quarters of an hour, then put the pheasant (previously three parts roasted) into the cabbage, and let them stew nearly three-quarters of an hour longer, or until the stock has partly reduced to glaze, and adheres thickly to the cabbage, when dress the cabbage in a mound upon your dish, with the bacon, cut into slices, around, and the pheasant upon the top, half way buried in the cabbage; have a little game sauce, which pour round and serve.

779
Richmond Maids of Honour

These delicious little cakes, which every inhabitant of London who pays a visit to the most picturesque part of its environs knows so well, derive their name from a period when cookery was not thought to be a degrading occupation for those honoured with that title. It is stated that they originated with the Maids of Honour of Queen Elizabeth, who had a palace at Richmond. I have a little work now before me, called 'The Queen's Delight', in which are several recipes invented by the wives of the first nobles of the land, which I think is an excellent example for those housewives who honour this book by their perusal, to imitate. They are made as follows:

Sift half a pound of dry curd, mix it well with six ounces of good butter, break the yolks of four eggs into another basin, and a glass of brandy; add to it six ounces of powdered lump-sugar, and beat well together one very floury baked potato cold, one ounce of sweet almonds, one ounce of bitter ditto pounded, the grated rind of three lemons, the juice of one, and half a nutmeg grated, mix these well together and add to the curds and butter; stir well up, filling the tartlet pans [and bake quick].

RECIPES

797
Apples with Butter

Peel eighteen russet apples, which cut in quarters, and trim of a nice shape, put them into a small preserving-pan, with two ounces of butter and three quarters of a pound of sugar, having previously rubbed the rind of an orange upon it and pounded it; pass them over a sharp fire, moving occasionally until quite tender, have ready buttered a plain dome mould, put the apples into it, pressing them down a little close; when half cold turn it out of the mould upon a dish, and cover all over with apricot marmalade; when cold it is ready to serve.

863
Soufflé Biscuits

Put the yolks of five eggs in a basin, and the whites in a copper bowl, add a pound of sugar, upon which you have rubbed the rind of a lemon previous to pounding, beat it well with the yolks of the eggs, then add a gill of cream, well whipped, and five ounces of flour; stir all together lightly, whip the whites of the eggs very stiff, and stir them into the preparation; have ready ten small paper cases, fill each one three parts full, and fifteen minutes before serving place them in a moderate oven; when done shake sugar over, dress in pyramid, upon a napkin, and serve.

874
Turban of Almond Cake Iced

This is a very good and useful second course remove. Make half a pound of puff paste, give it nine rolls, rolling it the last time to the thickness of a penny-piece, have ready blanched and chopped a pound of sweet almonds, which put in a basin with half a pound of powdered sugar and the whites of two eggs, or little more if required; spread it over the paste the thickness of a shilling, and with a knife cut the paste into pieces two inches and a half in length and nearly one in breadth, place them upon a baking-sheet, and bake nicely a very light brown colour, in a moderate oven; dress them on a stiff border of any kind of stiff jam or marmalade, so as to form a large crown, according to the size you require it; then fill the interior with vanilla cream, or any other, iced, but not too hard, and bring it up to a point; the cake may be cut in any shape you fancy, but never make them too large.

Select Bibliography

Boyd, L., *British Cookery*. 1976
Burnett, J., *Plenty and Want*. 1966
ffrench, Yvonne, *The Great Exhibition*. 1950
Goldie, Sue (ed.), *Florence Nightingale in the Crimean War*. 1987
Hankinson, Alan, *Russell, Man of Wars*.
Harrison, J.F.C., *Early Victorians*. 1971
Hartley, Dorothy, *Food in England*. 1954
Huxley, Elspeth, *Florence Nightingale*. 1975
Mayhew, Henry, *The Unknown Mayhew* (ed. E.P. Thompson). 1971
Morris, Helen, *Portrait of a Chef*. 1938
Quayle, Eric, *Old Cookery Books*. 1978
Russell, W.H.R., *Despatches from the Crimea 1854–56* (ed. Nicolas Bentley). 1960
Sadler, Michael, *Blessington D'Orsay* (Folio Soc. ed.). 1983
Sala, George Augustus, *Life and Adventures*. 1895
Sala, George Augustus, *Things I have Seen and People I have Known*. 1894
Strauss, Ralph, *Sala*. 1942
Tannahill, Reay, *Food in History*. 1973
Thomson, David, *England in the 19th Century*. 1951
Trevelyan, G.M., *English Social History*. 1944
Volant & Warren, *Memoirs of Soyer*. 1985 (facsimile reprint)
Wood, Anthony, *19th Century Britain 1815–1914*. 1960
Woodbridge, G. M. (ed.), *Early Victorian England*. 1934

NEWSPAPERS & PERIODICALS OF THE TIME, especially
The Times
Punch
Illustrated London News

CONTEMPORARY NOVELISTS, especially
Thackeray
Surtees

WORKS BY SOYER
Délassements Culinaires. 1845
The Gastronomic Regenerator. 1846
Poor Man's Regenerator. 1847
The Modern Housewife. 1848
The Pantropheon. 1853
Shilling Cookery for the People. 1854
Culinary Campaign. 1857

Index

Acton, Eliza 73, 74, 75, 76, 77
Ailsa, Marquis of 11, 12, 20
Albert, Prince 109
Ambler, Dr 150
Argyll, Duke of 131
Athenaeum, The 21
Atkinson, Ernest, *The Compleat Imbiber*
   No. 6 29, 30

Balaclava helmet 154
Barry, Sir Charles 24
Beauvilliers 70
Beeton, Mrs 74, 76
Biddulph, Myddleton 11
Bistros 69
Blackwoods Magazine 82
Blessington, Lady 111, 112
Boodle's 21, 22
Bornet 145, 146, 148, 150
Bracebridge, Charles 134, 138, 143
Brooks's 22

Cambridge, Duke of 11, 58
Carême 69
Cardigan, the 154
Carlton Club 22, 23
Cerito, Mlle Fanny 56, 60, 81
Charitable Cookery, see Soyer
Chesterfield, Lord 58
Chartism 3
Civil Aid Workers 147
Climate 8
Clubs 10, 21, 22, 23
Coachmen 5
Codrington, Sir William 151
Cole, Henry 109
Corn Laws 3, 43
Crimean War 126–129
Crosse and Blackwell 106
Culinary Campaign, see Soyer

Daily Telegraph 92
Délassements Culinaires, see Soyer
Dickens 7
Diet, changes in 8, 9, 11
Disease 128
Disraeli 116
D'Orsay, Count 11, 112

Duhart-Fauvet, M. Adolphe 93, 94

Ellice, Edward 22, 23

Francatelli, Charles Elme 72
   Cook's Guide and Butler's Assistant
   72
   Modern Cook, The 72
Fraser's Magazine 84

Garrick, The 21
Gas, Light and Coke Co. 25
Gaskell, Mrs 7
Gastronomic Regenerator, The, see Soyer
Gastronomic Symposium 115–125
Glasse, Hannah 73
Globe, The ix
Gore House 110, 111, 115, 118, 123
Gouffe, Jules, *The Royal Cookery Book*, 89
Great Exhibition 1851 13, 109, 110
Grey, Earl 34
Guardian, The 128

Halévy, M. and Scribe, M., banquet for
   62, 63
Harrison, *The Early Victorians* 6
Hartley, Dorothy 7, 8
Hill, Lord Marcus
   potage of 30
   ruling on Soyer 32, 33, 80
   in *Memoirs* 95
Illustrated London News 55, 77

Jacquets 61
Jones, Emma (Emma Soyer)
   early life 15
   marriage 16
Julien, cook 144
Jullien, musician 125

Lea and Perrins, Messrs 105
Lemolt, Chevalier 100
Liberals 22, 23
Lloyd, William 11

Melbourne, Lord 59
Memoirs of Soyer 11, 33, 46, 64, 65, 95
Modern House,wife, The, see Soyer

Montifiore, Lady
    The Jewish Manual 76, 77
Morris, Helen ix
Morrison, Peter 139, 146

Nightingale, Florence 128, 130, 131, 134, 138, 140, 141, 143, 153, 155, 156
Normanby, Marquis of 103

Observer, The 83

Pacha, Ibrahim 36, 37
Palmerston, Lord 36, 39, 40
Panmure, Lord 131, 132
Paulet, Lord William 134, 138
Phillippe, conjuror 59
Polignac, Prince de 2
Pückler-Muskau, Prince 87
Punch 42, 46, 62, 64, 106, 114, 116, 118, 122, 155

Radicals 22
Raglan, Lord, death of 144
Raglan sleeves 154
Railways 3, 4, 9, 10, 11
Reform Act 22, 34
Reform Club 12, 18, 23, 24, 25, 80, 115
    kitchens of 25–27
Restaurants 69, 70
Russell, W.H. 141, 147 153
Recipes
    Cakes, Almond, Turban of 175
        Biscuits, Soufflé 175
        Richmond Maids of Honour 174
    Fish Brill à la Purée de Capres 161
        au Naturel 161
        Herrings, broiled 169
        Mackerel à la Maitre d'Hotel 163
        Sole, Filets, en Salade 165
            Filets à la Reform 30
            à la Polonaise 161
            stewed in cream 75
        Saumon, à la Pecheuse 81
        Trout, à la Twickenham 169
    Game and Poultry,
        Capon, Poulade à l'Estragon 171
        Duck, Tavern-keeper's fashion 171

Fowl, fricassee of 173
Grouse, Salade of, à la Soyer 164
Pheasant, stewed with Cabbage 174
Volailles, Filets de, aux Concombres 164
Meat, Beef, fresh with Rice 130
    stewed, or Rump Steak 172
    to pot 170
Lamb, breast of, braised, boiled 170
    leg of, boiled, with Spinach 163
Mutton, Côtelettes à la Reform 27
    simplified recipe 29
    necks of, à la Legumière 163
    rognons de, sauté au vin de Champagne 162
Pork, neck of, Peidmontaise 171
Puddings, black, broiled 167
Veal, Noix de, piqué au jus 80
    Spring stew 75
Venison, hashed 162
Puddings, Abricots au Bavaroise 166
    Apples in butter 175
    Pommes à la Trianon 166
Sauce, à la l'Italienne 160
    à la Reform 28
    Orange, for Game 168
    Ravigote 168
Soup, Palestine 168
    Soup No. 1 44, 45
Vegetables, Bubble and Squeak 172
    Carrots, purée of white 169
    Cauliflowers and Broccoli 165
    Epinard au Jus 160
    Salade, French Family Holiday 173
Petites Fondues (en Caise) au Stilton 166
Syrup of Orgeat 152

Sala, George Augustus
    first meeting with Soyer 117
    friendship for Soyer 42
    catalogue for Symposium 117
    letter about Soyer 157
Sampayo 35, 36
Scutari, Barracks Hospital 128

INDEX

Seacole, Mrs Mary 142, 143, 154
Service à Table, à la Russe 88, 89
   à la Française 89
Simoneau, M. 15, 56, 58
Soyer, Alexis Benoist
   youth, 1, 2
   family background 66, 67
   in England 15
   dress 12, 13
   marriage 16
   on wine 31
   trouble at Reform Club 32, 33
   resignation from Club 41, 42
   in Dublin 47
   Philanthropic Gallery 53
   jokes of 59
   theatre and ballet 60, 61
   accident 64
   in Crimea 134–153
   illness 149–150
   death 150
   inventions of 97–104
   field stove 132, 146, 147, 151–154
   books by
      Délassements Culinaires 80
      Gastronomic Regenerator, The 73, 76, 80, 82, 83, 94, 95
      Charitable Cookery 54, 90
      Poor Man's Regenerator 47, 49
      Shilling Cookery for the People 90
      Modern Housewife, The 77, 82–84, 94, 99
      Culinary Campaign 5, 92, 129, 131
      Instructions to Military Hospital Cooks (pamphlet) 156
Soyer, Alexis II 66

Soyer, Emma, *see* Jones, Emma
   precepts for Ladies 17, 18
   pictures by 18, 19
   death 19
Spitalfields, weavers of, 50–53
Surtees, *Plain or Ringlets* 4, 10
Symposium, *see* Gastronomic Symposium

Thackeray, W.M. 12
   Pendennis 12
   as Goubemouche 42
Thomas 131 140
Times, The
   correspondence on soup 44, 46
   founding the Reform Club 22, 23
   Great Exhibition catering 112, 113
   letters from Soyer 51, 131
   letters on Crimea 128–130
   Symposium report 121
Traiteurs 57
Travellers Club 21
Tsar Nicholas I
   death of 133

Ude, M.
   disastrous party 71
   French Cook, The 72

Vatel 69

Wellington, Arthur, Duke of 69, 82, 83, 116
Whigs 22
White's 21

York, Duke of 58, 59.

Other titles published in the Southover Historic Cookery and Housekeeping Series:

William Verrall's Cookery Book
First published in 1759, with an Introduction by Colin Brent

The London Art of Cookery
By John Farley. First published in 1783, with an Introduction by Stephen Medcalf

The Complete Servant
By Samuel and Sarah Adams. First published in 1825, with an Introduction by Pamela Horn

The English Bread Book
By Eliza Acton. First published in 1859, with an Introduction by Elizabeth Ray

Series Editor, Ann Haly

SOUTHOVER PRESS
2 COCKSHUT ROAD
SOUTHOVER
LEWES
EAST SUSSEX BN7 1JH